# MIND YOUR LIFE

# MIND YOUR LIFE

MOIRAR M. LEVEILLE

# DEDICATION

I dedicate this book to my kind-hearted, sweet and beautiful daughter Brianna who is a total blessing in my life, my co-workers, and to whomever out there struggling to give meaning to the one life to live.

Life meant to live simply. Mind yours on earth to leave your mark. Know you are a gift to the world. Just believe.

# CONTENTS

# ACKNOWLEDGEMENTS

I WANT TO THANK SO MANY FRIENDS and family members, brothers and sisters, who kept on encouraging me and make me a stronger and better person. Thank you "Tio" Serge, my brother, for believing in the achievement of this book. Thank you to my dad, Raoul, always looking down on me, giving me the strengths of character to pursue my goals and believing in myself. You have always been there for us. Thank you to my mom, Lucianie Oscar, for teaching me, patience, kindness, understanding and persistence to conquer anything in life. Finally a deep and humble thank you to all my patients for your trust in me and for being my greatest teacher.

I love you all.

# INTRODUCTION

YOUR LIFE DOES NOT belong to you only. For true happiness you need to learn how to love to give. Develop that passion to win no matter what. You have time and energy if you want to accomplish your dreams. Nothing and nobody can stop you. Let go of your excuses, stop dragging your feet. Make your move to the right direction. Go, go, go.

Whenever you think about your mind, life and existence, you should think you have to stay focused, be committed with yourself, know yourself, know that life is a gift, follow your dreams, be grateful and always know that you are blessed. Envy is the bane of existence anyhow when really thought about deeply. When the grass seems greener on the other side, something it's rotten on both sides if you understand what that means.

For the ultimate value of a mind, a life and existence can be defined by how genuinely contained within themselves people really are without envious thoughts, without fearful oppression of conscience and without existing jealous of other people or situations.

So, view your circumstances as good, however they may seem to be and wherever you are with them, proceed with courageous thinking and know that your work stands well on its own. The best quality lives are judged on their own standards by the person living it. If you have to compare yourself to others in a genuine way, check your premises to use the words of Ayn Rand in a fully cognitive and rational way.

Real growth comes down to esteeming yourself well anyhow. Without that, you genuinely go nowhere except into envy and "keeping up". After all, why do you think "living like a reality show" is so popular for so many? "Keeping up appearances" is the weakest thing you can do. Being within yourself and fully understanding is the strongest thing you can do. This is not my opinion, but this is reality. Is there a self in the appearance without substance? There is not. But if you can have substance without the "appearance", that is better from a realistic standpoint because you (or anyone) are what they are "trying to be" in reality.

So, being blessed in that closed-minded way with control within yourself is the better way to be than appearing healthy and "great" in the eyes of others. Reality is what counts, not the hype of "the show everyone should envy."

Love without measure, laugh without a reason and sing without a tune. You are as powerful as you believe. Mind Your Life. If not today, then when?

# CHAPTER 1
# STAY FOCUSED

Y ou will change your life when you take the right steps, live well and take your life to the right direction.

## 1. YOU OUGHT TO LIVE AN OUTSTANDING LIFE.

Do you have any dream that you want to accomplish in your life? Do you want to live a successful life? If your answer is a yes, this book can help you to accomplish what you want and live the life that you desire. You are going to discover how you can achieve all your goals and your dreams. Lots of people are starting on the journey of self-improvement goals to enhance their lives and change their life around mindfully, emotionally and spiritually.

Your personal development is all about finding joy and peace in life, while growing as a fully actualized human being. This post contains a number of tips to assist you when you're thinking things like, I want a better life as you begin your quest for a personal growth plan. It is reasonably easy to overcome fears that are not unreasonable. A lot of fear stems from an absence of knowledge, so fight your fears by learning as much as you possibly can about them. When you're hounding yourself about, I want a better life, you might discover that your fears are unfounded, and that the subject of your fears may actually be more interesting than you had ever thought of. The majority of people are not living the successful life that they desire because they do not know how they can do it. Once you know the strategies and the secrets, you can achieve whatever you want in your life. Below are the 3 powerful strategies that used by successful people to achieve amazing results in their lives. Use them to produce the same results that you desire.

First, decide what you want in your life and stay focused on it all the time. Unfortunately, most people do not know what they want to achieve in their lives and this is the main reason they are living in mediocrity. Once you know what you want, you can then stay focused and think about it as much as possible. This will make sure that you will move toward your goals and are making progress every day.

Successful people have a clear vision and they think about it all the time. You must do the same. Second, create a plan and take consistent action until you produce the results you want.

Do you have a plan? Do you know what you need to do to achieve your goals? Successful people always know what they need to do in order to produce the results that they want. If you fail to plan, you will plan to fail. In addition, take consistent action each day to make sure that you are making progress toward your destination. If you are not doing anything, you will never create the outcomes that you want.

Finally, learn to love what you do. If you want to tap into your maximum potential to achieve great things, you must have a strong passion for what you do.

When you love what you do, you will do it with more commitment and you will do it with your heart. This is one the most important reasons that successful people are able to produce outstanding results in their lives. This is how you can unleash your greatness and the inner motivation within you.

## 2. HOW LONG HAVE YOU BEEN THERE? DO YOU KNOW WHAT YOU ARE WAITING FOR? START MOVING FORWARD TO REACH TO THE OTHER SIDE BEFORE YOU GO UNDER. JUST BELIEVE YOU CAN.

From all the events happening around us lately, without a doubt most of us feel overwhelmed about it. Some are within our control and some are not. Because of that, we tend to let those events take over and control us. We make those events the reason why we can't do this and can't do that. It's Time to wake up and move forward everyone!

We can't waste any more time and money being miserable. Instead, stick to leaders like glue. The type of leaders that would without a doubt, change you in a positive way. Become the person that people need. Stop always thinking what you need but start having the mindset of being concerned of what others need as well. Once we develop the leadership mindset, people will start coming for help and advice. You know the best thing about helping people? It just feels awesome! Helping people makes you feel so good. Sometimes helping people can become a selfish act. Why? Because it feels so good that you can't stop helping others. It's a good thing because it benefits you and the person you're helping at the same time.

## Only You Can Control What To Entertain In Your Mind.

Just because someone plants a negative thought in our minds, it doesn't mean we should entertain it. In fact, we should learn how to dominate it! Always remember, what we believe has a much bigger impact than what others believe. Have faith in yourself and start believing. If you don't then no one else will.

## Always remember that you are never alone.

There is always someone out there like us. Someone looking for change in their lives. When you are lost, never lose hope. Someone out there is most likely having things going way worse than our current situation. Instead, help others get out of their slump and create change instead of looking and waiting for it.

## Stop blaming yourself for your mistakes!

Instead, learn from them and grow as an individual. Don't ever make the past the reason why you can't move on in the future. Life is either an amazing gift or a horrible nightmare... it all depends on how you think of it.

**Time To Wake Up And Move Forward!!!**

Re-energize yourself and get the fire back! Don't ever stop until you get it back!

Don't ever waste time being stuck ever again. Instead, wake up and move forward! Today is another day... another day to improve yourself.

# 3. LEARNING TO LET GO IS A SKILL THAT CAN LEAD YOU TO SELF-DISCOVERY. THERE, YOU WILL IDENTIFY YOUR STRENGTHS TO CONQUER THE WORLD. OFTEN WE DO NOT GIVE TO OURSELVES ANY ROOM TO GROW. MIND YOUR DECISIONS TODAY.

You want to know how to let go? We all do at some point when holding on any longer is just too much.

You may want to know how to let go of a relationship that doesn't serve you or that causes you too much pain. Or to an addiction, to something that's not good for you...such as overeating, alcohol or arguing. You may want to know how to let go of a habit like biting your nails or being afraid to speak up.

There are a lot of things that people want to let go of. Here's the deal. They all have negative emotions at their core.

It's the negative emotions that are the "glue" that keeps you holding on and that prevents you from letting go and moving on.

A lot of people think it's your negative thoughts that keep you from letting go. But it's just not true. I can have a thought such as "I really don't care for Kerry's brother" that doesn't have a lot of energy associated with it. It's a passing thought about a preference without too much emotional charge. But the person standing next to me could have the exact same thought, "I really don't care for Kerry's brother," and it could be charged with anger, irritation, hatred or disgust.

Letting go of things that hurts is a way of starting a new life entirely. Brooding and worrying over past will continue to leave an unfilled space in your heart as well as give you questions with no answers. Let go of that thing that hurts you, the feelings, the setback, the worries, the failure, let it all go and start your life as a new soul. Only that way will you find happiness in yourself and you will realize how much you've missed yourself.

## HOW TO LET GO IN 4 SIMPLE STEPS

1. First, get in touch with the emotion you are feeling. You can't dissolve it if you run away from it.

Feel the feeling and answer the following questions with either a "yes" or a "no."

2. The first question is, "Could I let this go?" That means, "Am I capable of letting it go?" (And here's a hint, if you've ever let any emotion go ever, you ARE capable.)

3. Then ask yourself, "Would I let this feeling go?" And that means, "Am I willing to let it go?" (Don't worry, you can pick it up again later if you REALLY want to!)

4. And lastly, ask yourself, "When?"

This is an invitation for you to let go of that feeling right now.

Be sure to focus on your feelings as you do this process once through and then notice how you feel inside. Is the feeling a little lighter? Keep repeating this simple process several times until you can feel the "clutch" of the emotion give way. That relief or relaxation feeling is the energy of the feeling dissolving or unhooking itself from your thoughts.

There you go. You're on your way to freedom.

## 4. YOU DON'T KNOW WHAT YOU ARE MADE OF UNTIL YOU START TAPPING INTO THE POWER OF YOUR MIND. YOU ARE POWERFUL. MORE THAN YOU GIVE YOURSELF CREDIT FOR. YOU ARE AMAZING. SAY IT OFTEN ENOUGH YOU WILL BELIEVE IT.

We have all heard the stories of mind over matter and they are well documented enough to spur the medical and scientific industries to pursue it with enough vigor that has created technologies and methods that have allowed them to exploit the power of the mind. One good example of this is when a terrified mother is able to lift a car to free her child trapped in the burning wreckage. This is believed to be a common effect of the mind when placed in an environment of extreme trauma and emotions so that it amplifies strength.

This is the same logic that follows how some fighters are able to withstand extreme injury and even kill someone with a single blow when placed under duress. While our muscles and the physiological make up of our body has certain limitations, the mind does not, and often when the right conditions are met, the mind can gather all the potential power that a person has and focuses it into a single moment.

Pain is just another aspect where the mind is fully in control of, where pain receptors are activated when something injures you. But did you know that pain is simply a defense mechanism of the body to alert you that there is something wrong. While critical, it can be dispensed with chemicals like adrenalin and it can also be done away with proper meditation and preparation.

For example, we can take the fire walkers of India to be a potent example of this power. Not only are they able to walk on fire but the more stark example of their mind over matter is the fact that they are able to pierce themselves all over with hooks and spikes and carry large metal cages hooked onto their skin for hours on end and feel only minimal fatigue and pain. This is a prime example of meditation and the power of the mind to overcome anything.

This is what sets the normal from the extraordinary but the thing is, anyone of us has the potential to achieve this and control our minds to offset the limitations of the matter around us. We can do this either of two ways, either by enforced meditation, which gives us control over the subconscious mind and elevates us from physical limitations like pain and fatigue.

Or we can use technology, which has been developed to allow the entire population of the world to achieve this. One of the examples of this technology is brainwave entrainment, which uses the power of binaural beats to trigger the frequencies in the mind needed to give us the control we need over both the conscious and the sub conscious mind we have. Other examples of this type of technology also include bio-feedback, affirmation and autogenic.

The ability to transcend beyond our own physical limitations lies in the mind. You too can discover the ultimate power of mind over matter as most of these technologies are available online for your use— packaged as consumer goods in an affordable, easy to use medium.

## 5. PASSION DOES NOT LEAD TO TRANSFORMATION BUT ACTION. ACT ON YOUR PASSION AND YOU WILL TRANSFORM NOT ONLY YOUR LIFE BUT CONTRIBUTE TO OTHERS. THAT'S LIVING A MEANINGFUL LIFE.

If you set your mind to discovering and unleashing your passion the doors of opportunity will open themselves to you. Make it your purpose to find it and once you have found it, make it your purpose to follow it and you will surely succeed. Your passion might be raising happy, productive children, creating pottery, quilting or writing romantic novels. For some people gardening is their passion and for others it is fixing up vintage cars. No matter what your passion is, the important thing is that you find it and make the most of it. Your goal doesn't need to be being the best auto mechanic in the world; sometimes just doing the thing you are passionate about is enough to bring peace and satisfaction into your life. Following your passion can give you the fulfillment you need to get through any difficulties life brings your way. True success in life is being happy no matter what happens and following your passion gives you the opportunity to bring greater happiness into your life.

Passions are the keys to your destiny—they lead you to discover who you are and what you are here to do in this life. What are your gifts and what are you to do with them. When you align with these you begin to live a renewed life with boundless energy. You will be amazed as you begin to attract the things you need into your life.

What are you passionate about? Are you currently making time in your life to pursue your passions?

In general, what do you want more of in your life? What have you always wanted to achieve or do?

Were you at any point in your current work (whether employed or self-employed) passionate about what you are doing?

If so, think about what it was that gave you that feeling. If not, what were your reasons for choosing that particular job/industry or type of business?

When was the last time you felt energized by something you were doing? What were you doing? Where were you and who was around you? (e.g. teaching children how to watercolor, overseeing the fund-raising event for your church, managing the improvement project for the customer relationship management system at work).

Be open with your answers-- no boundaries here. Do not discount something you recall enjoying because it's not what's typically considered appealing. Write it all down.

Review each item on your list. What was it that you liked about the experience? What gave you that energizing feeling?

After you have done this for each item, find any common theme.

Circle or highlight the common words or phrases. This theme directly relates to what you are passionate about! Was your common theme teaching children? Teaching others about a certain topic? Were you around animals? I am not suggesting that everyone quit their day job today to find their passion unless that is a reality for you. Rather, start discovering what you are passionate about. If you are like so many of us who need the financial provision of a day job, start living your passion in small ways. Check out your monthly challenge below!

## Your Challenge!

Decide what you will do to experience more of your passion this month. If you're passionate about animals, but rescuing 6 dogs or starting your own parrot rescue nonprofit organization isn't a reality right now, what small step can you take to feel that you are making a difference in the lives of your favorite animal? For example, start volunteering one hour per week at your local shelter, or donate money to your favorite animal-centered charity. Take that small step forward and feel the fulfillment and passion you've longed for.

Your Passion—is the gifts you have or the things you love doing.

Your Purpose—as you focus on your passion, your purpose (opportunities to use your gifts) will emerge.

Find and do the things you are passionate about and you will never have to work another day in your life. What you do will be pure joy—more like a hobby or holiday than going to work.

How to discover your passion—Look inside yourself and find the things that make you truly happy—yes we all have them—look again, they are there. As they emerge, write them down and keep them where you will be regularly reminded. Spend a few minutes each day reflecting on your passions and you'll soon see opportunities dropping into your mind and your life as to how you can begin to develop your gifts, and how you can use them in service to others.

Along your path of discovery there will be those that will endeavor to discourage you. Do not let anyone steal them from you—do not be distracted. It is only by persevering that you will achieve and live out your passion and purpose.

Persevere if that first your passions don't emerge. Give yourself time and permission to explore this more deeply. Be kind to yourself as you embark on this journey. Reward yourself for early steps and achievements. It is a journey of realization which can take some while.

Sometimes we bury our passions deeply because of something that has happened in our life or out of the fear of what may be asked of us should we open this area of our life. We cannot open ourselves to our passion or our purpose until we are prepared to go beyond our comfort zone, scary perhaps, rewarding definitely.

Never underestimate the greatness that is in all of us.

## 6. WAKE UP WITH A PURPOSE. FOLLOW YOUR INTUITION. DECIDE TO START LIVING. DON'T PLAN TO WALK WITHOUT CHOOSING A DIRECTION FIRST.

What is our purpose in this life? Are we here to carry out the purpose our Creator gave us? But, what are you meant to do with your life whilst here on Earth?

There is a reason for our existence here on Earth. We exist to give value to others in our lives. It is true that once we know our purpose, there will be much more meaning of Life. Certainly, there has been so many questions of what Life can be. Life is made simpler when you understand the reason you breathe; there is an end for you to meet. You have been given life for the sole cause of fulfilling your destiny. You have a purpose to fulfill here on Earth.

We must all understand that there is a reason for which we were created. Get this straight everything on earth is for a purpose. The birds, cows and living creatures have their purposes for living how much Man, the crown of God's creation. Discovering should be the most important task you have. After you've done that the next thing is to fulfill that purpose. Sad to say there are lots of people who have not and will not discover their purpose let alone fulfilling such.

The question we then ask is why do we need to find our purpose for living? The answer is not far from the question. Knowing your purpose is the reason why you live. The reason why you are on earth. Why you are here. You don't ask a car why it was invented or ask what clothes are for. The reason is because we already know why they are there. As human beings our complex natures demand that we find out why we are on this planet. Now knowing your purpose does the following to you.

One, it simplifies our life, what greater joy we have knowing why we are here it helps us focus on the main thing and discard the nonessentials. Secondly, it gives us focus when you know your purpose in life you get to focus all your ability on it and guess what, you'll succeed.

Knowing your purpose motivates you, no other driving force is known than this. Lastly knowing your purpose gives your life a meaning, when you know your purpose you have a real sense for living which eventually gives you fulfillment.

When we do something with purpose, it is true that you do with determination. It simply means you have an aim or intention in mind. For example, the greatest purpose of a hammer is to hit nails. However, it is used by some people to reshape items such as hubcap or knock a table leg into shape. It shows us that the hammer has an ultimate purpose regardless other noble tasks. This can lead us to understand the definition or meaning of purpose. It is a reason which something exists or is used.

## So how do you know or discover your purpose in life?

Most importantly, you are a special creature who is valuable in so many ways. The Creator made you and deposited gifts inside you that no one else in the world can use in the same way and with the same quality you do. It's important however, to feel good about who you are, not just about what you do. It is the first thing you need to understand to discover your purpose.

A purpose does not search for the person, in fact the person needs to search for the purpose inside him/her and take it out to show the world. I believe, you need to go the extra mile to discover what is inside of you. For those who always say they don't have a purpose in life, they need to understand this. When you know what is inside you, you will be happy and aim to fulfill that purpose. "Spend your time trying to find who you truly are. Once you do that, spend the rest of your time showing the world who you are."

## 7. YOU HAVE BEEN BLESSED WITH ANOTHER DAY. STOP FOCUSING ON YOUR FLAWS. MAKE ONE IMPORTANT CHANGE IN YOUR LIFE TODAY. DWELLING ON YOUR CIRCUMSTANCES WILL NOT LEAD YOU TO FULFILLMENT. TAKE CONTROL TODAY OF YOUR DESTINY. TIME MATTER.

We all have our faults and failings. That is a statement of ordinary, honest fact. However, the vast majority of us mistake our inappropriate behavior for some inherent character flaw that leads everyone to whom I have ever posed the question "Are you 100% happy with yourself?" to immediately and forcefully answer "No!"

People will tell you they have "inadequacies", things they'd like to change about themselves. But when we dig deeper, two things become apparent. Firstly, our so-called inadequacies are not real, they are perceived, this perception arising from how we were made feel about ourselves during our formative years. Secondly, the things we'd like to change about ourselves are either generally behavioral or the result of our behavior.

No one is inadequate—though many of us feel a great burden of inadequacy. Vast swaths of psychological work and research, stretching back over a century at this stage, indicate that we are the product, or some would go so far as to say, the victim, of our upbringing. Indeed, I have found, with every single one of my private clients, that their self-perceptions are the direct result of their interaction with people and events during their formative years. As a result, even those with the happiest and most loving childhoods developed into "normal" adults— "grownups" who are not entirely happy with themselves. As a result, they live lives with which, at the very best, they are not entirely happy—or, as most people say "not too bad". Surely, not too bad is not good enough.

Our perceived inadequacies are etched on our deep subconscious mind as a result of a process called "snapshot learning"—when an event takes place that makes a great impression upon us, that's exactly what happens—a deep impression is printed into our subconscious. Snapshot learning generally only takes place during our formative years— particularly up to the age of 11 or 12 years, with the final touches being added during adolescence—anywhere up to the age of 25 years. After that, we, generally speaking, have very fixed views about ourselves— very fixed views of our own inadequacies.

When set out in the manner in which I've done so above, we can immediately see the stupidity of dwelling on our inadequacies—they come from a past long gone, but one on which the subconscious mind is continually, daily focused. What is of at least as much concern, however, is that those same out of date snapshots create—and, daily, re-create—the repetitive, automatic, reactive behaviors that result in us doing things that we'd prefer not to have done. Bad habits, snapping at people, manipulating those we claim to love, losing our temper... make out your own list.

The big problem is that when we display those daily faults and failings, as I said already, we mistake our automatic reactive behavior for ourselves—we perceive ourselves as in need of repair—and, as a result, not only do we beat ourselves up, often becoming frustrated that there is not easy exit from the apparent continuous treadmill of the same reactive behavior. Some resort to bad habits that will help them come handle or suppress their feelings—I've come across alcohol, drug and sex addictions—all of which, clearly, only make matters worse.

What we've got to realize is that if we stumble and do something stupid, destructive or hurtful, that's all it is—a stumble. Replaying the stumble, feeling guilty about the stumble or being certain that there's no way out of stumbling again are all useless thoughts that add to our own incorrect feelings of inadequacy, low self-esteem and lack of self-worth. When we stumble, we need to stand up, dust ourselves off, pull ourselves together and start over.

But that's only part of the solution—because if we just do that we may never learn from our stumblings—we may never rise above our perceived inadequacies and the manner in which they automatically create our stumblings. We need to break out of the automatic mode in at least 96% of people live—validated by years of research. Quite obviously, this is done by being mindful rather than, through automatic behavior, being totally mindless.

Mindfulness comes from paying attention to the present moment—to what your body is telling you about now, through your five senses. This may sound simple—and, yes it is, but it's not easy to practice. In fact, you'll take a lifetime perfecting your ability to be attentive to the here and now but, in doing so, you will drag your subconscious mind's attention away from past snapshots and prevent those past snapshots dictating the kind of automatic reactive behaviors that make you unhappy.

In developing your ability, through the deliberate and conscious use of your five senses, to give more and more of your attention to the here and now, you will see the here and now for what it is—one moment in time, where you can choose to be "all there" and do your best, or you can choose to abdicate responsibility for your own state of mind and let the automatic programmed subconscious alter ego repeat past mistakes. The choice is yours—moment to moment. In deliberately exercising the choice to be more attentive to the moment, you will see your perceived inadequacies for what they are—illusions—and see the real you for what you can be—here and now.

## 8. RENEW YOURSELF. DECIDE, COMMIT, ACHIEVE. YOU HAVE WHAT IT TAKES TO CHANGE YOUR LIFE. DON'T BE IN LOVE WITH YOUR PAST, IT DOES NOT MISS YOU. BREAK UP WITH YOUR MISERY. START BELIEVING IN YOUR ABILITY. ISN'T IT TIME?

What about you? What's your life story? We've had good times and bad times, too. There have been times you were happy to be alive and some days you'd like to forget altogether. There's nothing wrong with that-it's part of the human experience. The problem is allowing your past to determine your present and your future.

Your past is your history. You can't go back and change things, no matter how much you wish you could. You can't always be re-living the great times, either. It just doesn't work that way. What you can do is change how you think about it. You can accept life for what it was in that moment but realize you have to live in the present. You don't have to let the past determine who you are right now. You can reinvent yourself any time you're ready.

People live in the past for different reasons. It's up to you to decide what you're going to do with today. Are you going to live in the past or are you going to live in the present? Will you let your past be your future, or will you decide to change your life's course? You can't be positive about the present and future while focused on the past. Let go. Enjoy what you have today and what you will have tomorrow. Focus on your dreams and forget about the movie reel playing the collection of the worst of your life. Surround yourself with eagles who encourage you to live the life you've imagined. Believe in yourself and let others have faith in you. Things you've done or things other people have done to you? You can't change it. The issue is your attitude about what happened. How do you let it affect you now? Whatever memories or experiences there are, you have to make peace with them. If you won your high school championship, be proud of the fact-and move on with the rest of your life. If you've lived through a tragedy, you don't have to let it define you-it can simply be something you experienced. You must learn to move on.

Moving on includes getting over what you and what other people have done to you in your past. We all love to receive a compliment, but what sticks with us are the hurtful words people have said over the years. You may receive a hundred compliments, but they're all going to be drowned out by the one criticism.

You can't let other people's opinions of you keep you down. You get to choose your own life, regardless of what happened in the past and what others think of you. You can move on with your life, even if others don't believe you have or you can.

You don't have to bury your past-you just need to come to peace with it. When you speak about an experience, you can talk about the good that came out of it and how it helped you become who you are today.

Write down the experiences in your life you haven't gotten over yet. Decide what you need to do to come to peace with them. If it's counseling, get it. If you need to apologize, do it! You can't fully live until you've come to peace with your past.

Past Life Regression can be an effective tool in overcoming many situations where you are feeling stuck and out of sorts. For instance, do you ever get the urge your life is set in a repeating pattern and things are just one re-occurring cycle? Feel like you are trapped inside a situation where you can't seem to find your way out and no amount of hard work on your part is seeming to get the results in life you are looking for? You are not alone!

Being stuck in a continual loop is frustrating at best, and can be devastating to deal with. It wastes valuable life time having to deal with the same issues in various forms over and over again, especially when you feel like you should have learned the valuable lesson the last time around.

In many instances, Past Life Regression can be a valuable tool in overcoming those devastating highs and lows and can allow you to function at the level of prosperity God meant for you to have in your life.

How does Past Life Regression work? You don't have to believe in Regression for this Therapy to work. Simply allowing the healing process to go forward and recognizing the link in the debilitating behaviors associated with your actions is enough.

It works like this, Past Life Regression allows you to link yourself to patterns you have in your life which are carried over from mistakes you have made in past existences. By searching back into the time those patterns existed, they can be recognized and released, breaking the cycle that has been created in the current life. Even if you do not believe in the process, Past Life Regression acts very powerfully in helping the mind understand why you carry those debilitating behaviors with you in the first place.

"Remember that it is up to you to choose every day to get off Your Attitude and to create a positive lifestyle for yourself and others". Believing in yourself lets you gain confidence that others may not have in you otherwise. People are naturally attracted to others with a strong self of themselves in friendships, relationships, family and jobs. Those who don't have a confident personality eventually tend to drag others down unintentionally because it's difficult to be around a person who constantly has a gray cloud hanging over their head.

If you don't have self confidence in yourself right now, make the choice to gain it right now. That's all it takes to take a step forward, a choice. This choice to believe in yourself end up causing a domino effect and spills over into all facets of who you are. Now, make a list.

What makes you great? Everyone is different, so when making your list, make a list about you. If you have trouble making this list and find yourself wishing you more like so-and-so, make a list of the attributes of that person, but don't become someone you are not.

If there is any iota of doubt that keeps creeping up and hindering you from moving forward in life, all you have to do is tell yourself, "I can do this!"

This simple statement will give you the confidence to push through the challenges to be successful in your endeavors. Niggling doubts and fears will be stomped out firmly just with the power of believing in yourself.

Many times in life, we grow up with a set of beliefs. These may be influenced by our childhood experiences, the atmosphere we have grown up in, or some particular events that have been transformational.

Some of these beliefs really motivate a person to get ahead and achieve all that they want; but some beliefs can also be severely detrimental.

Limiting beliefs can put a person behind in life. You may come across scores of such people who lack the courage or determination to achieve a target, just because they do not believe in themselves. In fact they are always looking for excuses not to pursue a set target, because they find it discomforting to break the mold that they have built around themselves.

If you do not want to be counted in this group of individuals, you have to trust the power of believing in yourself. Do not listen to those voices in your head that make you fearful whenever you think of making a bold decision, because those are your limiting beliefs.

Instead, tell yourself loudly that you can accomplish anything, and stop those negative thoughts right where they begin! They are always the culprits, and they try very hard to sabotage your attempts at going ahead with your plans.

All you have to do is simply erase these restrictive thoughts as soon as they emerge and immediately replace them with positive thoughts. It may not be automatic at the start; but if you do this often, you will find this practice gets easier each time.

When you constantly motivate yourself and fill your head with positive thoughts, you will see the negative and impairing thoughts becoming weaker and weaker; and eventually, they will make an exit from your life!

If you are able to combine the power of believing in yourself with the right doses of courage and determination, you will see significant changes in your life.

## 9. FEAR: IS IT KEEPING YOU SAFE OR LIMITING YOU TO GROW? ASSESS, DECIDE, AND STOP COMPLAINING. MOVE BEYOND YOUR FEAR TO REACH GREATNESS. TODAY IS A DAY TO SAY ENOUGH. I AM MORE THAN THAT. I AM CAPABLE. I AM POWERFUL. I AM LIMITLESS. I AM FEARLESS. I AM STRONG. I AM GROWING. ALLOW YOURSELF TO MOVE ON FROM YOUR MISERY AND BECOME THE ONE YOU MEANT TO BE. DON'T SEAT AND WAIT. YOU HAVE BEEN THERE FOR TOO LONG WAITING...MAKE THE FIRST STEP. THAT'S ALL IT

# TAKES. ONE STEP AT A TIME.

There is nothing to fear but fear itself. Isn't fear enough? Do other cultures use such catchy quotes? Per Webster "Fear—an unpleasant, often strong emotion caused by expectations or awareness of danger." Not only can fear be "unpleasant", it can be destructive and downright debilitating. Dread, panic, terror, trepidation. There are many faces of fear and all elicit a feeling of un-ease. Everyone has fears: of failure, rejection, and abandonment. We're human!

Fear may in fact have benefited early civilizations by signaling danger, triggering fight or flight, and ensuring the survival of our species. Today, when our basic survival needs are met, fear can stop in to rob us of a peaceful and fulfilling life.

We were fear-free as children. How do we get that back? Mark Twain suggests courage. Courage is not the absence of fear; it is control of fear, mastery of fear. Great concept!

You take a moment to reflect on what you have achieved in your life. You realize that some of your plans have not been accomplished yet. Its time to stop dilly dallying. You don't have to live your life in regrets. Old age slows down your life, but that does not mean you need to limit yourself to activities you can do. You can still live the life of a youth. To spring start you, revolutionize your outlook. Be daring no matter what. You will not live your life to the fullest if you let your fears hold you back. To get over them, start by making a list of things that frighten you. Just let your mind flow freely as you jot them down. Avoid analyzing them. Hold your list, and study your fears right from the very top. Find out what bothers you for each particular fear. Then, clarify what actually troubles you. Obtaining a thorough understanding and more experience about what scares you is very vital for you to get over it. Because your knowledge and self-confidence improves, you minimize the possibilities of your fears and concerns infringing on your life.

Living a youthful life also requires that you learn how to be contented with what you possess. You will never be at peace if you are constantly seeking perfection. You will be chasing after wind if you always wish to have something in a certain way. Dissatisfaction and discontentment also comes if you always focus on the negative. That doesn't imply that you shouldn't give your life your best shot. Although there will always be a better way to do something, you need to learn how to enjoy and appreciate the ways things already are. Guard against this horrible habit of persistently wanting things to be your way. Tenderly, remind yourself that life is just fine the way it is presently. The more you give up your need for constant perfection, the more you will discover the greatness of even the small things in all aspect of life.

Courage is the ability to move beyond your fears to conquer what is right and moral. It is to stand up for yourself; not to be bludgeoned by negative rhetoric and theories that remove the gift of self-empowerment. Standing up and feeling secure in the face of adversity is an awesome task, but made much easier when you recognize all the help that is available for you, both on earth and in heaven. Feeling courageous comes much more easily when you absorb the alliance between yourself and the angels that surround you.

If you are going through a stage in your physical life where you feel overwhelmed and underappreciated, it is the best time to show the strength of your loving convictions. Moving beyond consciously and subconsciously created worries, doubts and fears will not only make you a being of courage, but also someone valued highly by society. In addition, your efforts to plow through your tests in life are dually noted by the Ascended Masters. They will help to create more opportunities for you to devour all that troubles you and replace it with the positive aspects that the universe stores for you. Remember, you are completely worthy of NOT struggling. Life can become one of simple tastes; of simple love.

For those who are going through health challenged times, we are here to say to you that you need not worry about how much time you have left. Instead, focus on what you want to achieve. Whether it is perfect health or fulfilling something you want on your list of life goals will be guided and assisted by the courage you muster. Fear of dying is often the largest reason for people not to heal because the focus is on the outcome you prefer did not happen. As we are always telling you, the universe brings energy to the aspects of your life that you give the most attention to. It is not naïve to visualize and expect a healing! Envisioning and creating a mental movie of the desired outcome is nothing more than programming the universe to tune into that channel so you can feel rewarded. No one is ever overlooked or forsaken, especially when they show a courageous demeanor and attitude towards working for something positive and optimistic.

# 10. IF YOU ARE GOING THROUGH SOME PAIN, OR DIFFICULTIES DON'T STAY ALONE. IF YOU ARE IN THE DARK, FIND THE LIGHT. BE DETERMINED. NEVER GIVE UP. YOU HAVE MORE THAN YOU THINK TO SUCCEED. YOU MIGHT FEEL LONELY BUT YOU ARE NOT ALONE.

It's very easy for us humans to go through some type of frustration. When it comes to pursuing a goal, we don't really know what to expect. We don't know how it is going to challenge us or even change us. Sometimes, it's a lot easier to give up. We convince ourselves that the situation we're in is unbearable we lose sight of our main objective.

### Never Give Up! Remember Why You Started In The First Place

If we forget why we started in the first place, then the problems that we're dealing with becomes almost unbearable. But if you think about it, how much would we really appreciate something if we could attain it so easily. Perhaps a struggle is necessary to prove to ourselves and to the world that we want to succeed no matter what. Randy Pausch once said,

"The brick walls are there for a reason. The brick walls are not there to keep us out; the brick walls are there to give us a chance to show how badly we want something. The brick walls are there to stop the people who don't want it badly enough. They are there to stop the other people!"

No matter what the rest of the world says, you should never give up on your dreams. In your young years, you possess so many goals, and you feel that all is possible. However, as you age, most of those dreams get pushed away. Yet, if you give up, you end up living an unfulfilled life full of regrets.

Do you think that you do not have what it takes? Perhaps you believe that your vision is impossible to realize? Why should you think that? Did you take a shot and fail before? Did somebody tell you that it was not possible? Is it that the probabilities are too high?

Well, no matter what is your age, situation, or difficulty, you should never give up on your dreams. Maybe friends, relatives or people around you said you should stop making a fool of yourself. Doubt steps in and fear begins to take over. And yes, it can look unpromising, but is it why you should let go of your dreams?

Nothing is more ordinary than unsuccessful people with talent. You must know that determination and persistence are godlike powers. Nothing in this world can stop you if you have these two attributes. Just as education, talent, and mastery, they can be learned and applied if you have the real desire to go after what you want.

And yes, there are times in your life when the challenges seem overwhelming. You got hurt by a few successive setbacks and obstacles, and you feel like throwing in the towel. But know that there are people out there, who are in fact enduring, persisting and working through the challenges to achieving their dreams. They have learned to do it silently, step by step, day by day. They have patience, and no matter the time it may take, they will not give up on their dreams.

**Dreams as Marathon Rather Than Sprint:**

You do not often hear the stories of people before they become famous. Most people choose to give up on their desires the very moment they are facing an obstacle or two. Is it crazy to think like that? Of course, it is. It is even stupid! But how could I judge? I am not judging; I am stating a fact.

To cut a long story short, imagine you decide you want to go and see a relative. So you prepare a few things because that family lives four hundred miles away from where you live. You then get in your car and begin to drive. You pass the first hundred miles, and then another, and another, but suddenly when only one hundred miles away, you get discouraged. So you decide, then and there, just because you are not at the destination yet, to give up and return home.

You understand. You should not give up on your dreams because the success you are waiting for might just be happening tomorrow, in a week, a month or even a year. You invest in yourself, put all that hard work in, so trust me, you are special, and it will pay off in the long run. Realize that you are running a marathon in spite of the fact that you assume it is a sprint.

**The Necessity of Never
Giving Up on Your Dreams:**

Often, many of us think it is a quick dash. Countless people say they want to accomplish great things. They have the wish to change the world. But then, whenever they are facing terrible circumstances, challenges, barriers or even failure, they get unmotivated, and most of them quit on their dreams.

You have to stop and think that the journey is worth more your while than the destination. It is the best tactic to stick and never give up on your dreams, goals, wants, and desires. You have to keep going when the going gets hard and slow, and you will see it through.

Of course, on the other hand, some people believe they are failures and give up on their wishes from the start. They do not get out of their comfort zone and prefer to procrastinate every day. What goes through their mind on a daily basis? One might wonder.

Wait a minute! In fact, they do dream and wish, but they are so busy going out, drinking, partying, hanging out with friends, watching television, or looking for attention. They are even so busy that they forgot about themselves and the necessity to improve. So they come up with various excuses, and then they say that the world is against them.

### The Options of Giving In or Never Giving Up:

Most people get too accustomed to laziness. They have no problem doing the things that are easy and fun, but when it comes to the hard and demanding, they run. Therefore, you are left with two options.

## GIVE IN AND HAVE REGRETS:

You have to realize how unbelievably easy it is for you, me or anyone to form unhelpful and harmful habits. But when the need to develop positive habits comes into play, such as the concept of never giving up on your dreams or anything that matters, it takes you a much longer period.

These additional efforts make you wonder if you should not stay away because these conditions make you feel pretty uncomfortable, and you do not want that. Who would? You could just wait and see what the future brings. You might be lucky enough and be able to trick life once more.

You have nothing to lose, right? Nothing, except your life, your time, and perhaps your happiness. But that is not a waste. So, in the end, when you will look back on your life, and you will see how much you have accomplished, and the regrets you will have, you wished you had never given up on your dreams.

## NEVER GIVE UP ON YOUR DREAMS:

Realize that time passes with you or without you. If you think that your dreams will take too long, you might be in the same place where you now are, thinking if you should start. Of course, beginning on such a journey may take days, months, even years, but do not let that stop you from taking the first step. It might seem impossible at first, but if you do not start now, you will never achieve it.

Plenty of stories abound about people that never gave up on their dreams and defied all odds at all ages. If you think you are too young or too old, it does not mean you can or cannot do something. It all starts in your mind. No matter what, never give up on your dreams, and do not let your age stand in the way of chasing after your desires.

Consider the author who started a new career at 50 years old. You may also think of Sylvester Stallone, who created the "Rocky" films. His idea was rejected countless of times before somebody finally offered him a chance. And in the end, determination paid off.

# THE REASON TO NEVER GIVE UP ON YOUR DREAMS:

The reason why you should never give up on your dreams is that you, I and anyone else have something that makes us all unique. You have particular expertise and talents. So, stop comparing yourself to others and focus your attention on all of the things you have but do dismiss.

The line to success is never straight but rather unconventional. A part of the process is to hit bumps in the road that look like walls, to make mistakes because if you do not, you are not trying. In history, numerous well-known figures have failed time after time.

Therefore, you never know what can happen. Doubt and fear are the greatest killers of dreams. What if you fail? But what if you succeed? Is that reason not enough to never give up on your dreams?

Our body and mind are wired in such way, since thousands of years, that it is always easier to imagine the worse. You have never thought that perhaps the opposite could be true? Why should you let anything stopping you from trying? You have the right to become the best version of yourself. So, never give up on your dreams!

### Tips to Not Let Go of What You Want

- Never surrender your precious dreams, because one day, you will accomplish them.
- Work on taking the necessary action steps in that direction.
- Get motivated and inspired by people who never stop trying like Edison or Lincoln.

- Keep focused, and you will eventually achieve your dreams.
- Believe in yourself, work for it and never give up on your dreams.
- Avoid negative influences that sow seeds of doubt.
- See failures as lessons, as opportunities to grow, improve and master.
- The harder it is, the more worthwhile it will be when you do it.
- Avoid the fear of hard work and go for it.
- Realize that the only person standing in your way is you.
- Choose not to listen to people telling you that you cannot do it or it is impossible.
- Prove the non-believers wrong by not giving them the satisfaction of seeing you give up on your dreams.

You can accomplish great things, but you have to never give up on your dreams. You must commit to your goals, your desires, and what you believe in. Abandon your beliefs about what you can and cannot do. Each day is a new chance for you to begin, make new choices, learn new things, meet new people and improve yourself.

Simply imagine being able to rejoice with your loved ones, relatives and friends who have been there for you since the beginning of your struggles. Think about the feeling of pleasure you will have. When you cross the finish line knowing that you accomplished your goal because you decided to never quit on what you wanted, it will provide you with an unspeakable sense of victory. Now, go and do never give up on your dreams, no matter what, because success is yours.

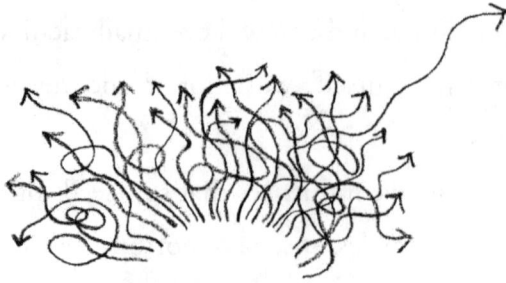

## Chapter 2

# BE COMMITTED
# WITH YOURSELF

**M**OST PEOPLE FAIL not because of a lack of desire but because of a lack of commitment. Commitment is the foundation of great accomplishments.

**1. BE COMMITTED TO CHANGE ONE BAD HABIT TODAY. STOP THINKING POWERLESSLY. VICTORY IS YOURS. THINK IN YOUR ABILITY TO MAKE LASTING AND POSITIVE CHANGES. BELIEVE IN YOURSELF. LET GO OF YOUR PAST TO**

# MOVE TOWARDS YOUR DESTINY NO MATTER WHAT. TRUST YOUR INSTINCT THAT YOU'RE CAPABLE. FOCUS ON YOU.

Accepting change has always been a difficult task for most people, since they are reluctant of letting go of the comfort that they are used to. When you choose to affirm yourself positively, you can end up either in avoidance or in reappraisal. If you find yourself resisting change due to negative feelings or fear, it is because your subconscious mind is trying to avoid the challenge of dealing with the change. You can affect the way you perceive things by having positive affirmations that you have to repeat continuously and believe. This will create a conviction for you that will slowly fight off your resistance and finally; you will ease yourself into the change you feared.

Affirmations work by redirecting your thought frequencies and patterns hence replacing your negative beliefs with positive ones. You change the way you think and the way you feel about things, and you start to see tangible results of your positive affirmations. Affirmations will work for you if you are ready to leave the past behind and embrace a new way of doing things so that you can free yourself of the negativity that has been subconsciously subjected to you.

Whenever you are trying to tell yourself something, either by thought or by saying it out loud, you are affirming yourself of something. We are constantly affirming ourselves to do something, change something or achieve something. All our affirmations are a manifestation of our inner beliefs and truths. Most of the affirmations we have are acquired at a tender age, hence they are deeply rooted in our subconscious mind as we grow. Most of our responses to every situation are an automatic adaptation from the way we were raised. This is because our subconscious mind uses memories, feelings and everything that has been stored over a period of time since we encountered it.

The affirmations we have are a great impact on the way we perceive things and the world in general since they affect the way we react to everyday events. For us to survive, we have to adapt to the environment. Learn to react quickly towards the events that take place around us and be able to examine everything that is around us. Most of the affirmations we can be dated back to the foundation of our lives during our early ages. It could be beliefs that we learned from our parents and the environment from which we first understood the way things work. Therefore, some of us may have negative affirmations acquired from the environment, their parents or their experiences. However, you can acquire positive affirmations through subliminal messages that are manifested in the subconscious mind without the knowledge of the conscious mind.

Positive affirmations are used by the conscious mind to change any negative attitude that we might have grown up with in our subconscious mind. They are usually in the form of positive statements that you have to keep repeating and believing so that they can replace the negative attitude that you are trying to get rid of. Positive affirmations have been reported to work very well in helping people to get over their fears, achieve many goals, change one's focus towards a positive future, accept change, and many other positive outcomes.

Is there a change you tried to make but have not succeeded? Why people, in general, experience extreme difficulty when trying to change a single habit? What changes should you start with?

It is not an easy question. Making or creating a 'different' you can be tremendously challenging. But if think your life is currently on the wrong path, or not where you want to be, then a radical amount of constructive change in positive ways might be the best thing.

So, to change yourself requires a lot of discipline, but also knowing what your 'ideal self' looks like and recognizing your current weaknesses. It is usually a time when you take a hard look at the truth and realize that enough is enough. That is why it is uncomfortable for many people to make a change.

## Beginning to Change Yourself

No one ever said it was going to be easy! To reach your ideal, you need to find role models who will help guide you along the way. If mentors are absent, read books about people you admire and begin to copy their habits. To change yourself, you need to have short and long-term goals.

In my life, there are so many changes I have gone through. And no matter if the change was small or big, each time was of importance. Studies show that to change a habit takes around 21 days, so three weeks. Yet, I had habits that took months or years to change as they were ingrained more in-depth into my unconscious.

Therefore, realize that you might be different. It may be easier or harder depending on the change or habit. You have to figure out what works for you. With that said, if you want to make a difference and develop different and new habits, start first by believing you can.

## How to Change Yourself in Positive Ways:

Learn from the best when it comes to transforming yourself in a different you. Again, find people who truly embody the person you want to be. Use and imitate various qualities or habits you respect from different persons to make a change. But you have to develop positive ways of thinking. It is the first essential key to help you replace, build, and form any other habit or change you have in mind. Of course, positive thoughts alone will not lead to straight to success. On the other hand, it certainly assists you in pushing you to do the things required to succeed.

So, if you allow yourself to have negative thinking, you always end up failing. You have to think positive thoughts instead; it will give you a higher chance of success. It could be invaluable to you! Practice positive thinking again and again, until you can change and form just about any habit you need.

## Change by Taking Baby Steps:

The key to change is making baby steps to imprint a new habit into the subconscious. Every goal or change you make should be a step toward your desired outcome. Small changes or goals should be tangible, but do not be afraid to have a big crazy goal.

Then, focus on only one small change. When you focus on one habit or goal at a time, it is more efficient. It is a powerful way of achieving your goals or changes for that matter. Focus and energy are the two vital ingredients for making a necessary change or the desired objective.

Therefore, pick one of the habits to focus on first. Break it into smaller aims and choose an action you can do today. Keep doing it every day until your goal is accomplished. Then get to the next modest target and so on. In some instances, turn them into habits until your routine is ingrained. And then focus on the following goal to achieve.

## Change of Daily Routine:

Change seems simple, and yet it is hard. You need to transform and create a new daily routine for yourself, which will make an enormous difference in your life. It means developing a habit for the morning, afternoon and evening.

Thus, it will revolutionize your life because a new routine will help you to simplify your days, focus on what is most important, and build the life you desire. In short, you have to eliminate the non-essential in your life.

First of all, you need to identify the things in your life that are most important to you, or what you love the most. Then eliminate all other stuff. It makes things simpler and gives you the space to focus on what is essential.

## Cultivating Kindness as a Change:

Yes, cultivating and being kind is a great habit to have. Try to focus on kindness each day for a month or two and see what sorts of profound changes enter in your life. It will change you in positive ways, and over the long run, you will see people act towards you differently and even treat you better.

It is called karma! How can you cultivate a kindness habit? Well, first, make it your goal to say or do something kind for a living being each day. It does not matter if it is human or animal. During the day, when an opportunity presents itself, be kind or do a caring act.

Therefore, each time you talk, interact or work with somebody, make an effort to be kind and compassionate. Finally, attempt to go beyond and into more significant acts of compassion. You could volunteer to help those in need or animal causes.

### A Final Word on Change and New Ways:

So, begin to change your wrong habits in positive ways and accept any small success. Each time you reach a short goal or transformation, you get closer to your outcome. It is a great thing!

However, do not get too satisfied when it happens. Take some time to appreciate the change and keep moving forward to your next desire. These new habits will change your life. It will help you genuinely root the constructive changes in your everyday life.

Push and drive yourself to become a better version of the person you are now. To change yourself in positive ways and get better habits, you need to have a vivid picture of your final goal and then break it into smaller goals. And then, let it become a routine that gets ingrained and becomes a natural part of you. I know you can do it!

# 2. DO YOU KNOW WHO YOU ARE? THEN HOW CAN YOU LOVE YOURSELF? START HAVING A RELATIONSHIP WITH YOUR-SELF FIRST. MAKE EVERY EFFORT TO FOCUS ON YOUR

# STRENGTHS WHILE WORKING ON YOUR FLAWS. YOU ARE MORE THAN JUST THAT. START BELIEVING IT. IF NOT NOW, WHEN?

John Donne, the English poet, once said: *"No man is an island."* Yes, in a way, we are all related to other people in our lives--whether we are at home, work, or play.

Relationships are at the core of human existence. If you understand other people in your life, you will develop better and more positive relationships with them. Understanding people means knowing how to react to them in certain situations, leading to good human relationships. Having good human relationships is the art of living well.

But understanding other people around you may not be easy, especially if you do not understand yourself first. By understanding yourself better, you may be able to relate better to other people in your life. Therefore, the key to the art of living well is knowing yourself first.

## Why is knowing yourself so important?

Above the doorway of an ancient Greek temple were written the words "Know Thyself." The significance of those words was: Knowing yourself first! If you know yourself, you need not even ask the oracle for a prediction of your future. That is to say, if you know yourself, you could answer all your own questions in life. If that is the case, why do you bother to ask the gods? Just ask yourself--you hold the answers to all your questions in life.

Who are you? That is the question you should ask yourself first, rather than what is going to happen to your life.

Your Creator has created you for who you are and what you are. Your worth lies within you, just as Ann Frank said, "Human worth does not lie in riches or power, but in character or goodness." If you believe in the goodness in yourself, you would know how to treat another individual you encounter in your life. If you know yourself, you would know what another individual would want. Dalai Lama, the spiritual leader of Tibet, was once asked by reporters how he could so easily and instantly relate to people of different cultures, religions, and backgrounds. He promptly replied that he was "simply encountering a fellow human being with the same desire to be happy and to avoid suffering as myself." In other words, an acute awareness of the needs and wants of any individual.

Indeed, if you know yourself well enough--to know who you are and what you want from life--you would know how to deal with another individual with the same needs and wants as yours. Essentially, treat others as you would like to be treated. The problem with many of us is that we simply don't know ourselves, and therefore we don't know others. As a result, we don't know how to react appropriately in certain circumstances, or how to treat others just as we would like to be treated.

Then, how do you know yourself? The best way to know yourself is to meditate. Meditation is a mental process during which your mind focuses on something seemingly insignificant and irrelevant, such as your breathing, so that you can explore your subconscious mind to find out your real needs and priorities in life. Many religions advocate the practice of meditation as a means to enlighten the mind and enhance spirituality. Meditation is easy to practice: it requires only discipline and diligence. Use meditation to know yourself, thereby knowing others in your life. Knowing yourself may surprisingly solve many of your life problems.

In order to succeed developing a satisfying intimacy you first need to develop a relationship with yourself

Having failed until now might mean: you haven't yet taken the time to develop a relationship with yourself: to get to know yourself better; to understand the ways in which you harm your attempts at relationships; to realize a host of factors which might control you and lead you to sabotage your attempts.

Reading these lines you might tell yourself, "What nonsense, I do know myself, don't I? I know who I am and what I want" . But you might be surprised to hear that many are not aware of "who they are" and of the ways in which they sabotage themselves and their relationships. Many—you might be included—live their life and "do relationships" on automatic pilot, without ever asking themselves if there is anything they need to change in order to succeed with their relationships. Many tend to blame others for their failures, or to believe that they haven't yet found their "soul mate".

But the truth of the matter is, that as long as you don't take the time to develop a relationship with yourself—with self-compassion and open heart—you might not become empowered at developing the intimate relationship you so much desire.

## What does it mean "to develop a relationship with yourself?

Developing a relationship with yourself means: taking the time to look inwards; to get to know "the person that you are"; to see whether you have been authentic with yourself and with others; whether or not you are walking around with masks which deter you from being "who you are"; whether or not you are driven by fears, needs which weaken you and influence your reactions and behaviors with prospective partners in an unhealthy way; whether or not you are controlled by unrealistic expectations and fantasies about partners and relationships, which drive you to react and behave in your relationships in harmful and non-constructive ways.

Developing a relationship with yourself means, becoming intimate with yourself; learning all you can about your denials and projections; realizing the hidden agenda you might have had until now regarding the ways in which you presented yourself to yourself and to others.

When you develop an intimate relationship with yourself you become empowered to develop an authentic and healthy relationship with others.

## Developing a relationship with yourself requires commitment

Developing a relationship with yourself requires a commitment on your part: a commitment to go ahead and find out "who you are" and what was it that stood in your way from developing a successful intimate relationship until now.

The best way to develop a relationship with yourself and become aware of "who you are" is to do so on a friendly basis: as you look inwards you let things reveal themselves to you; you accept them with an open heart and explore them with compassion.

Being committed to look inwards, explore and realize how you have shot yourself in the foot until now, enable you to become intimate with yourself and therefore empowered to develop an intimate relationship with another.

Knowing yourself is a very important task which one has to undertake, it can often be the most challenging as well. When a person knows who they are, and clearly understands what they want, then they have a much better chance of discovering how to reach their own success, happiness and personal fulfilment! Knowing one's true inner self can be of great help to anyone working to reach their goals more effectively. It helps guide you along the path toward success. This not only fills us with much happiness, bliss and calmness but also improves our mindset, as well as our relationships and connections with others. Knowing yourself consequently, empowers and enables you to create different choices. Success easily comes to those with pleasing personalities.

However, this does not necessarily mean that you must do everything which other people want you to; rather it means acquiring a positive attitude and mindset... it means being respectful to the opinions of others while at the same time remaining true to one's own beliefs. Don't expect to suddenly go on a certain course and immediately become aware of yourself or enlightened. The success of such a journey depends deeply on how bravely you face yourself; on the way, you might discover certain things which you do not like and possibly choose to hide or even deny. Be strong and accept those negative things because it is only by admitting and accepting your faults, that you can truly change them for the better.

Be open to accept and listen to the opinion of others, eager and willing to learn. Changing your judgment and views on account of more reliable facts is not a sign of weakness—but of strength in your character. Always be inclined to offer help, be caring and polite while at the same time keeping your own personality... The basic principle of knowing yourself is that every person is responsible, in control and generate their own thoughts to the life they encounter. This is a process which may at first seem complex and may well be severely obstructed when one is unaware of how one functions, or if one has a misunderstanding of their true nature.

Rationalizations are used by many people to give a justifiable explanation for their actions. One may then pretend that the problem is not their own—and now it may be blamed on the other person. This is known as projection. You therefore need to discover and improve the true you, and not what others perceive you to be, and also not who you believe you must be, but the person that you truly are. Develop enthusiasm in yourself. Enthusiasm not only draws good relationships but also success. It is that positive outlook that radiates from you, which will make other people like dealing with you. Your positive and enthusiastic outlook will contaminate and encourage those around you to also become enthusiastic and positive; therefore fully cooperating with you.

Also, be ready to face unreasonable and negative people and never let them effect your positive emotions. Try to stay both reasonable and calm. Knowing yourself will enable you to develop your full potential and be happy, contented and fulfilled. Whether your idea and understanding of success is fulfillment in business, friendship, love, sports, a blend of all these or another thing altogether, knowing yourself and working on change for the better will enable you to achieve your goals!

Then indeed, when you reach your goals, you will turn out to be a much happier person. And that is real success in its truest sense.

## 3. YOUR LIFE IS A RESULT OF YOUR THINKING. WHAT HAVE YOU BEEN THINKING ABOUT LATELY? CHANGE YOUR THOUGHTS TO CHANGE YOUR LIFE. YOU HAVE CONTROL OVER WHAT YOU THINK TO CHANGE HOW YOU FEEL. YOU CAN ONLY ATTRACT WHAT YOU FEEL.

How much do you think your thoughts influence what happens in your life? You've read that question and now you are thinking about it in a conscious way. As a consequence of that you are forming an opinion on it. That's how powerful thoughts can be!

Most people aren't fully aware that their thoughts bear such a strong influence on their daily lives. But once you start to think about it, you will see that it's true.

Let's look at a simple example to prove this point. Let's say the garbage truck is coming round tomorrow morning to collect the rubbish in the neighborhood. If you think 'I must go and put my garbage out ready to collect' this will ensure it gets collected. If on the other hand you think you can't be bothered to do that, you'll be living with lots of garbage around you until the next collection comes along.

Put simply, the nature of your thoughts will affect your external surroundings. We've looked at an example involving garbage but we can apply the same principles to lots of other situations in life as well.

## Are you starting to see how important it is to have control over your thoughts?

Ensuring your thoughts are positive ones:

You can probably see quite clearly now that your thoughts do indeed influence your surroundings. You are probably looking round right now and seeing more evidence of this. You might think you'll tidy the house later, so you're living in an untidy one right now!

Luckily we do have full control over our thoughts. It can take time to get used to thinking positively all the time. But when you do you will start to notice it becomes a habit—and it brings about lots of great events in your life as well. Better things will start to happen more regularly. You might even start to feel 'lucky'. Although of course we already know that positive thinking is responsible for that.

The first thing you have to do to change your life for the better is to become aware of your thoughts. Get into the habit of doing this as soon as you wake up. If you let yourself think negatively from the get go, you will often find you're thinking like that for the rest of the day.

So start as you mean to go on. Focus on positive thoughts and monitor yourself throughout the day. If you feel a negative thought coming on, block it and turn it around. As time goes on you will find it gets easier and easier to think positively without even realizing you are doing it.

You should also become more tuned in to what is happening in your life. Gradually you will start to notice changes in your life—changes for the better. They may not happen overnight but if you continue to think positive thoughts they will happen.

## Doesn't that sound like the best way to live your life?

You can only think one thing at a time, and unless you are sleeping, you are always thinking something. This is what gets us in trouble, but at the same time, it is also what gets us out of trouble. The truth is, learning to control what you think When you control your thoughts you control your life.

If you can change your thoughts, you can change your life. It makes no difference what your life is at the moment; you can change it for the better through your thoughts. Our thoughts determine what we are experiencing and what we will experience in the future.

We do not realize the tremendous power of thought we have. Through the power of thought, we can be in control of our lives. (As a man thinketh.) When a negative thought floats into our minds, immediately cast it down and think something else. (Chinese proverbial saying "You can't keep a bird from flying over your head, but you can keep it from making a nest in your hair.") You are in control of what you think about.

Your mind is never blank—you are always thinking something. From the moment you open your eyes you begin to think. But what are you thinking? When you think negative thoughts you will speak negative words. You will speak what you think. Your thoughts can change your life for the better.

Your thoughts will change your actions. If you think a certain way, you will act that way. Good or bad. You act on what you have thought about. Your thoughts precede your actions. You cannot do anything without thinking it first. Our actions are a direct result of our thoughts. If we have a negative mind we will have a negative life.

You need to begin to think about what you are thinking about. That dominant thought you hold in your mind—is it good or bad? So many people's problems are rooted in thinking patterns that actually produce the problems they experience. You will produce what you are thinking about. In other words, the problem you are experiencing you are experiencing it because you thought about it for so long it has materialized; it has happened.

When you change your thinking, little by little you will notice your life starting to change for the better. When you begin to think rightly your conditions will begin to change.

Eleanor Roosevelt was famous for a lot of things. One of the most inspirational words she ever said was, "No one can make you feel inferior without your consent." You are what you are; you and only you are responsible. You may not believe it but it is very true that you can use your thoughts to change your life.

You come across choices every day. It is the choices that you make that can make the difference in your life, the big difference between failure and success. What are the thoughts that go through your mind when you are confronted with these choices?

Do you really have the right thought process at work? Do you really have the right mindset? If your mind is not thinking right and your thoughts are convoluted, do you think you can ever achieve what you want in life? Do you think you can ever attain your goals if your thought process is not precise?

And so, because you have the wrong thoughts about the way things are and the way they should be, you do not get what you want in life. Slowly but surely, you begin to think negative. You think of yourself as a failure and more negative thoughts fill your mind.

But remember this great Yiddish proverb, "Do not make yourself low; People will tread on your head." Never think lowly of yourself. Never ever make the mistake of thinking that you are not as good as the other "guy".

You have to change the way you think. You have to fill your mind with thoughts that are only the best and the highest. You must Use your thoughts to change your life. Think good and you will achieve greatness. That is the key to success. Give it a shot!

Did you know that if you use your thoughts you can really make a difference in your life? You can really change the way you think and make things better for yourself. Are you stuck in a dead end job? Do you feel like your life could be better? If this is you then now is the time to change the way you think and start thinking positive. The power of positive thinking is priceless, therefore start putting your mind to changing the way you think.

# 4. WOULD YOU BE PROUD OR EMBARRASSED IF A MICRO-PHONE WAS IN YOUR HEAD SAYING OUT LOUD WHAT YOU ARE TELLING TO YOURSELF? HAVE RESPECT FOR YOUR-SELF. TREAT YOURSELF KINDLY. MIND YOUR THOUGHTS THEY BECOME YOU. DECIDE TO BE NICE TO YOURSELF NOW. YOU ARE AMAZING. LOVE YOURSELF ENOUGH STARTING TODAY.

There is a world out there based on love and respect, and it all starts with you and me. We love naturally because it came with our being and upbringing. Otherwise, it's up to us to learn. Many parents are great at instilling in their children to love life, and that's ideal. But to love and respect yourself, I think it takes practice. Like an artist focuses on improving his or her talent, may it be in: singing, painting, playing a violin, a cello, a trumpet, they all had to work hard at it.

The amazing thing about loving and having respect for yourself is that it follows one of the most important rules of human behavior. If you just consider the history of mankind, you would find that had love prevailed in the hearts of men, instead of hatred, prejudice, and envy, millions of mostly young soldiers and civilians of all ages might have lived their lives through.

St. Paul put it so clearly when he said, "But now abideth faith, hope, and love, these three; and the greatest of these is love."

If we were to apply love to everything, I believe that life would be so much more beautiful. But life is a reality and not an illusion, and we all face trials and tribulations. Many people have a difficult time coping with life, and loving and respecting themselves is not what they strive for.

As parents, friends or work companions, we can easily make an appreciation of people just by the way they dress. How they behave is a different matter, but when it comes to loving one self, the clothes that a person wears in public say a lot. For example, when people are down and out they tend to wear 'gray-dull clothing' and they look untidy. When they are happy to be alive, they lean towards 'bright-colored clothing' which reflect their joy and excitement. The first thing you will notice is that they keep themselves neat and clean all around.

Here are some excellent suggestions to help you stay in love with yourself, and to respect yourself every day of the year. I consider them the "best ways" because they are easy to follow and truly fun to apply.

1) **Exercise to your heart delight.** It is the best medicine for a broken heart, and especially when you feel down and out. There is no end to exercising the body because it can take a lot of punishment. Indoor and outdoor workouts are good for you. Looking fit physically produces a joyful state of mind.

2) **Loving yourself means controlling your weight.** Being overweight is not healthy for you, anymore than being too thin by applying "starvation" diets. Try and balance your correct weight according to height and age. A proper diet and steady exercise are the answers to a better body.

3) **Take the outdoors for all its worth.** The sun is not a bad thing for your skin if you put the proper lotion to protect it. The sun provides health and vitality for you. Enjoy it when the sun is out and shining. It brings life and energy to everything, and you will get a chance to get out of your house or apartment for a spell.

**4) Grooming is essential to a healthy lifestyle.** Untidy people give the impression of dislike and lack of respect for themselves and life in general. Choose clothing that help you to look and feel happy and younger. You want to control your moods, and allowing for 'drab clothes' to dictate your day will simply not help you to like, or even less, love yourself.

**5) Don't let work and home be the only activities in your life.** Make it a point to go out and see a concert, ballet, opera, jazz, play pool. Expand your horizons, and try and reduce the hours that you watch sports all year long on television. You want to become a participant in sports, and not a full-time spectator that many people choose to be.

**6) Make the world a part of your life and not a "foreign place forever."** You can bring the world to you by studying the different cultures, languages, music, history and foods. By opening your parameters you will open up your heart. Loving is sharing and learning, and it all starts with you.

**7) On your birthday, make it the most joyous and celebrated day of the year.** Why, you ask? Because it shows that you love and respect yourself. It's that important! There is nothing more beautiful than to be called on the day that you were born by family and friends. That means that they remember and love you. That's what life is all about! Kindness is reciprocated by you calling them on their birthday also.

You will always find love in everything around you when you see the good and the beautiful in people and nature, but especially in yourself. Life is long enough for most people, but death is unpredictable.

No one knows when it might creep up on us. So let us waste no time in making life a whole lot better as of right now.

Love, on the other hand, is predictable. Make loving yourself your goal throughout your life; and despair, anxiety, and unhappiness will have no room in your heart, your life, and your daily thoughts. Follow that with self-respect, and you will have gained what many people need to strive for: self-confidence, dignity, and a good dose of self-esteem.

If learning to love yourself is difficult, I will give you the secret to getting there faster. Like everything about you first. Make it a point to say good things to yourself on a daily basis; and as you develop a habit of complimenting yourself every day for any small or big thing that you do, you will enjoy liking everything about you. That's when you begin the path towards becoming your own best friend.

As you develop a liking for yourself, you will find that respect for your person will also rise in almost direct proportion. In time you will reach the point when the transition is made from liking to loving yourself. When that day comes, celebrate it with your family and friends.

It's obvious that in various parts of the world, people want with all their heart to be happy and loved. It's not a mystery, but it is a journey of searching and finding that happy medium, that balance between your daily life of work and struggle and a moment of peace.

As you strive towards attaining 'unselfish' self-love, not vain love, you will bring more happiness to your life and to those near you than you can ever possibly imagine. The results are inevitable, and all that it will take to get started is a good look at yourself in the mirror and decide that change is good. That's love and self-respect looking at you, and begging for you to initiate the beginning of a new and a wonderful life.

Stay up with information on how to stay happy, cheerful, and content with tips and recommendations by visiting "Cheer Up World! Learn the Best Ways to Happiness in Your Life." You will find the site next to my name.

## 5. BE COMMITTED TO LIVE IN A STATE OF MIND THAT CAN HEAL YOU NO MATTER WHAT. GIVE YOURSELF PERMISSION TO BE HAPPY TODAY. START LIVING LIFE IN YOUR OWN TERMS. IF NOT TODAY, THEN WHEN. BE EMPOWERED

Clearing or Healing your mind can be started with a process that is similar to accessing the task manager on your computer by typing control then alternate then delete to access the task manager of the computer of our minds. We are not conscious of all of the memory files that our brains have stored without our awareness because your brain is always working. It is always running tasks and it never stops working.

Your subconscious mind never stops running. It is like the computer program constantly running until we configure it. But first we must access what's running with our conscious minds. Knowledge is the key to change because it is in your conscious knowing that you access the ability to configure the hardwiring of your brain to change your subconscious mind programming and habits.

We literally need to hit the ctrl+alt+delete buttons of our minds to control then alternate and delete thoughts and programming that has hard wired your mind for inferiority. Just like a computer program, there was a certain point in time when the program was downloaded in to your subconscious brain and started this ceaselessly running process.

This is why scripture says my people will parish for lack of knowledge. Because when you cease to learn your mind and body, they continuously run a destructive program which makes you like a ticking time bomb designated for self-destruction. Your mind needs healing.

Most people want to change their life situations and their environment, which is likened to the production of a computer and how it runs, by trying to get rid of their minds computer virus by screwing screws in the pc and shaking our monitor and not once do they consider downloading a mental anti-virus program in their minds to produce change.

Second you need to gain control of the process of healing your mind. This one step seems to be so out of the reach for most people because most people cannot understand one of the first processes in gaining control, which is quieting down the mind. You have to access you're past programming by clearing the loud noisy mind and letting the silence speak.

You should realize that you own time and time does not own you. Slow down! We are to in a hurry. We want to finish so that we can accomplish our goals in a hurry. Well your goals can be more reachable when you operate on a different plain. This plain is the dominion of control. To control a light switch you have to know how to operate the off switch.

Then as your mind and body realize the silence it will send you signals of the programming that is deeply lodged into your souls patterns. It will come up into your frontal lobe and reality will take place. You then can alternate what's there. You then have the ability to analyze it from a spiritual level with the open third eye that penetrates all things.

Then you will see and know the truth about healing your mind. You will be aware and your higher self will be the rightful judge to sentence the thoughts with complete and full justice. Then if need be then you delete the memory file from the mind. But you have to understand where the program came from and know its specs. You have to have the understanding of what programs to leave running and what programs to clear.

This knowledge will come from beyond your personal reference. It will come from beyond your memory bank that judges the unknown or any new situation at hand by your perceptions of pain or pleasure. Time and space is at your power and service when you learn how to use the control+alt+delete button for their brain to access the programs running in our very big and powerful mind. Here is where you manage the task of your creation!

Here is where the area of healing or clearing the mind taken place. A healing energy comes from silent nothingness. Some people have mastered this healing and harnessed it as energy healing. Energy healing is a way to clear your mind because everything is energy.

Millionaire affirmations are energy fields, that permeates and penetrates the cells of your body and attract money, money, and more money the more you affirm millionaire affirmations into your millionaire mind.

No matter what's taking place in your life, it's always possible to heal and transform your mind. You never know what great potentials await you just around the corner. Here are some ways you can let your greatest difficulties be your greatest allies for uplifting your life and making sure you move to higher and higher ground.

## 1. Keeping the Faith may be the Way to Keep on Keeping On.

Once when I was undergoing some difficult times, I wrote to a spiritual teacher about it, and he said, "Times may be difficult now, but with your faith and your devotion, your life will be transformed." This became the way for me. I knew that there was such a thing as "divine timing" and that everything would open up for me at the right time. So I kept telling myself that it was all getting ready to break through for me. And lo and behold, life opened itself up for me, and I was able to move forward. The same is happening for you.

## 2. Plan It; Imagine it; Hold the Space for It.

Let your imagination help you plan the next steps. It's important to accept what's happening in the moment, but it's also of great benefit to imagine the potentials for yourself. Some people have never let themselves imagine what could be possible. Go ahead and let yourself do it. Get ready for a transformed life. Even in the midst of difficulties, get ready for everything to shift for the better.

### 3. Affirm It.

Speak positive words about the potentials for your life. Don't give the time of day to your complaints or self-pity. Speak words of possibility. You too can say, "I AM the resurrection and the life." You can also say, "I AM the power of healing and I AM healing myself now." You can say it over and over, using these words instead of negative ones.

### 4. Get Ready for a New World.

While it's important to "be here now" and to accept your current say of viewing your reality, it's also important to project the potentials for a transformed world. While some people say that 2012, for example, is going to be the cataclysmic end of the world, others say that something quite different can be expected. There is the possibility that there's an optimistic interpretation and that it's the end of the world as we've known it. It could mean the rebirth and transformation of humanity in which we all know universal love and peace.

# 6. "I AM" DO YOU KNOW WHO YOU ARE? TAKE A MINUTE, START YOUR SELF-DISCOVERY, SET YOUR STANDARDS. LET GO OF SELF-PITY AND THE BLAMING GAME. RENEW YOURSELF. IT TAKES TIME TO KNOW YOU, HAVE SOME DISCIPLINE TO DISCOVER YOUR TALENTS AND YOUR TRUE POTENTIAL. BE COMMITTED WITH YOURSELF. MAKE TODAY A BETTER DAY THAN YESTERDAY. STOP WAITING FOR MIRACLES; MAKE MIRACLES HAPPEN IN YOUR LIFE. YOU ARE THE ARTIST OF YOUR LIFE. START YOUR CARVING...COMMIT

# TO ONE ACTION TODAY TO KNOW YOU. THIS IS A NEW DAY AND THE FIRST DAY OF THE REST OF YOUR LIFE.

Each one of us is a unique person. We have different bodies and different talents, but your self is uniquely you.

Yet your self is not a thing that can be seen or touched in the outer world. It is not a fixed state that does not change. It is the dimension through which you experience your life. It is an evolving process that grows throughout your life. It transcends the composition of your physical body (which turns over its physical ingredients regularly). It is a pattern that transcends its parts, just as your face can be recognized as a pattern that transcends your eyes, nose, and mouth, and just as a melody can be recognized as a pattern that transcends musical notes. However, because it is multifaceted, you experience yourself through its parts rather than as a whole. For this reason you cannot experience all aspects of yourself simultaneously. Still your emotional comfort and psychological integrity depend upon your awareness that you have a whole self.

The easiest way to envision the pattern of your self is to build up a mental picture of it by describing its parts: your 'me', your myself, and your I. The personal pronouns me, myself, and I are very special words indeed. They have no synonyms.

The terms me, myself, and I refer to demonstrably separate parts of yourself. Simply put, your 'me' is your person, your 'myself' is your mind, and your 'I' is your self-awareness.

## Your Me (Your Person).

Your 'me' is your physical presence, your skills, and your personality that distinguish you as a particular person. It casts your external image in the perceptions of other people and of yourself through your visible appearance and actions. It is the only part of yourself that you can see in a mirror. Your 'me' relates you to the outer world.

Your 'me' is reflected in your conscious awareness by your sensual perceptions of the outer world, of your emotions, of your bodily sensations, of your instinctual drives, and of your body image. Your 'me' contains your cravings for physical gratification, security, and power. As such, the inclinations of your 'me' are to use other people to satisfy your own needs and to fight or flee when your own needs are threatened. Your 'me' contains your "false selves" that you have learned as accommodations to the expectations of others. A false self will be defined later.

Although your 'me' aims to ensure your survival as an individual, your me cannot be de-pended upon for satisfaction with your life. In addition it can create problems for you by demanding unattainable security, by becoming obsessed and bored with material possessions, by competing with others for power and control, and by urging impulsive actions.

## Your 'Myself' (Your Mind).

Your 'myself' is your mind. Your 'myself' consists of mental imagery of your outer and inner worlds. It is composed of your conscious and unconscious thoughts, your imagination, your dreams, your knowledge, and your conscience. It includes your beliefs, your values, your self-concepts, your evaluations of your own personal qualities, and your judgments of others.

## Your True Self.

The core of your being lies a powerful, loving, creative nature—your true self.

You are born with your true self. It contains your genetic potential. It is the source of your creativity, the perceiver of your sensuous perceptions, and the site of your spirit. It is the source of your capacity for unconditional love; of your capacity for integrity; of your capacities for truth, beauty, and justice; of your capacity to experience moral guilt; and of your capacity for self-esteem. Your true self is remarkable indeed!

Knowing your true self depends upon making what may still seem to be a fine distinction between the terms sensuous and sensual. Yet that distinction is crucial to understanding the sensations that you can use to become acquainted with your true self. This is because your access to your true self is through your sensuousness.

In order to fully understand the difference between sensuous and sensual, you may well need to go against the way in which you have been conditioned to think.

Unfortunately, our society does not help you become aware of your sensuousness. One of the basic problems in our society today is the failure to distinguish between sensual and sensuous experiences. This is most clearly seen in confusion about the meaning of the word love. Is love a sensual (physical) or a sensuous (spiritual) experience? It is no coincidence that confusion about whom and how we love actually reflects confusion within our own selves because we do not know how to distinguish between our sensual and sensuous experiences.

Discovering and developing the sensuous experiencing of your true self is not easy in our contemporary society, which does not encourage the appreciation of natural rhythms, pleasures, and discomforts. We are preoccupied with the sensual stimulation and discomfort relief provided by commercially produced machines, by machine-made items, and by events of the outer world. As a result we have come to believe that the products we purchase are superior to the sensuous experiences that occur naturally in our inner worlds. We find ourselves spending money, sometimes lavishly, in the quest of satisfactions that money cannot buy. We find ourselves turning to the stimulation of movies, television, and computers for excitement and pleasure rather than drawing upon our own creativity.

Our society fosters satisfying immediate sensual pleasures rather than savoring sensuous satisfactions. Both political and commercial purposes can be served by gratifying our sensual urges. Appealing to pleasures, fears, and pains is a sure way to manipulate people to serve one's purposes and to buy one's products. We are bombarded with continual sensual stimulation by events in our outer worlds. We find it difficult to reflect peacefully in our inner worlds. Consequently, we become bored easily and seek the continual stimulation of work, recreation, and chemical agents. Some of us compulsively indulge our sensual urges in mechanical ways, as in excessive eating, smoking, drinking, and sexuality. We become conditioned to seeking sensual gratification. And that is good for business.

Because of the sensual orientation of our society, you may well be unaware of the vital distinction between the intangible experience of sensuousness as beauty by your I and the tangible experience of sensuality as the bodily gratification of your me. But you can become aware of the differences. When you are under the sway of your sensuality, your life revolves around the appearance of your 'me' in the eyes of others and around maintaining a desired public image. When you are in tune with your sensuousness, you are responsive to the inner world experiences of your 'I', and your life revolves around your spirituality. Your capacity for sensuality favors a materialistic orientation to life, whereas your capacity for sensuousness makes it possible for you to develop a spiritual orientation to life.

You may not realize it, but one time that you sensuously experience your inner world is when your creativity holds sway, as when you use a tool in an art or craft. The satisfaction you experience from a creative thought or act is sensuous. While tools extend your creative use of your hands and senses, machines can either replace or enhance your creativity. For example, computers can do tasks for you as machines, but they also can extend your creativity as tools.

This brings us to your true self. The psychologist Abraham Maslow described the true self as the source of sensuous, aesthetic experiences in the form of truth, beauty, justice, coherence, simplicity, and creativity. Contact with your true self takes place through subtle feelings, such as inner peace, inspiration, self-confidence, integrity, and effortless activity. Expressing your true self takes place through the unconditional loving of others and through harmonizing conflict and diversity. In the quiet center of your true self you also can discover the truths that lie in the fundamental paradoxes of life.

More specifically, the two sensuous experiences of moral guilt and self-esteem are vital clues to expressing your true self. You and I have the innate capacity to experience authentic guilt when we are not fulfilling or are betraying our potential. That twinge of guilt, although uncomfortable, can be a growth-producing clue that you and I are not fulfilling the potential of our true selves. Moral guilt, more than social guilt that arises from our consciences in our 'my selves', can be a wholesome, monitoring influence in our lives. It can help us to improve our lives.

Just as there is a crucial difference between sensuous and sensual, there is an important difference between what we should do and what we ought to do. Doing what we should do con-notes doing the proper thing with respect to other people. The voice of your conscience tells you what you should or should not do, revealing its origin outside of you in the expectations of others. Right and wrong are determined by values you learn from other people. Your conscience gives rise to social guilt. For example, you feel guilty when you do not do what you are supposed to do, such as attend a particular religious service. Because social guilt is not authentically our own, we tend to have ambivalent feelings about responding to it. It can mire us in pointless self-recrimination and depression when we feel we are imperfect in the eyes of others and therefore in our own eyes. That kind of social guilt can be stultifying and inhibit spiritual growth.

In contrast, doing what we ought to do connotes moral obligation. Moral guilt reminds us of the things we ought or ought not to do. Moral guilt reminds us that we are imperfect and can do better. It stimulates growth in our spiritual journeys.

The feeling of self-esteem also is a cue that you are in contact with your true self. Self-esteem results when you value yourself, when you nurture your talents, and when you accept your imperfections. You experience self-esteem when you appreciate your own worth and when you accept accountability for your own shortcomings.

Our true selves are the parts of ourselves that contain our innate talents. They are the sources of our creativity. Although we will never fully know our true selves, they are exciting realms of continual discovery throughout our lives. Therein lie both our challenges and our fulfillment in life.

## False Selves.

Just as ancient Greek actors wore masks (personas) while performing, we wear the masks of our false selves in order to maintain the outer world images we have learned to show in our various social roles. An obvious example is when we act differently in our work places than we do with members of our families in our homes. Our personalities include these necessary false selves first learned in our childhood roles, so that we do and say the appropriate things expected of us in particular social situations. The parts of ourselves that show to other people are our false selves.

Each of our false selves is expressed by behaving so as to maintain a particular image in the eyes of others. Our false selves are necessary social adaptations, because we all have reasonable expectations of each other. Certainly shopping goes better when store clerks act courteously even though they are tired and eager to go home. We are well advised to observe false self-etiquette in social situations.

The term false self is an appropriate description of one of our external faces, because it is in accord with the fact that you and I are imperfect human beings engaged in a lifelong struggle to discover and to express our true selves while living in an outer world that necessitates social accommodations. The term false self also helps to explain why you and I do feel false at times and why some of us are actually known as "phonies." Your challenge and mine in life is to imbue our false selves with as much of our true selves as is possible.

That challenge is becoming increasingly imposing. The technological advances and changing lifestyles of the last century now expose us to many new social roles. One of the effects of this social overstimulation has been the generation of new roles for ever-expanding audiences, such as father, stepfather, son, stepson, brother, husband, ex-husband, student, teacher, friend, athlete, team-mate, patient, client, customer, seller, employee, boss, taxpayer, voter, expert, critic, performer, patron, parishioner, driver, passenger, contributor, writer, reader, victim, perpetrator, foster parent, foster child, adoptive parent, adoptive child, and so on. As you can see, each one of these roles brings out a different aspect of yourself.

Do the many roles you play contribute to stress in your life? Isn't it likely that this is true if the motivation to play a role comes from the outer world rather than from your inner world?

Our false selves are based on our own and others' perceptions and are defined by what we and others can see, hear, and touch. They are superimposed on our sensuous true selves. A particular false self usually arises in compliance with the expectations we imagine others have of us. However, it can be expressed in opposition to the expectations of others, as does a rebellious teenager. It can be a reaction to distortions of how other people perceive you, as does a shy person. Or it can conceal unacceptable parts of yourself, as does a pious person. A false self also is subject to lapses when "others are not looking."

A false self lacks full authenticity because it is primarily determined by our social obligations and by our psychological defense mechanisms rather than by our true selves. It tends either to assume the characteristics of the person upon whose expectations it is based or to assume the opposite. Therefore, we are likely to have ambivalent feelings about a false self. It may be overly compliant with others' expectations, or it may differ too much from others' expectations. This explains why we can have conflicting feelings about the ways in which we play our roles in our vocations and in our family relationships. We may even be confused about what others expect of us because others can be unclear about what they expect of us as well.

Our false selves can confuse and destroy relationships when they are not grounded in, and monitored by, our true selves. When our false selves are out of touch with our true selves, we are like a machine playing out recordings prescribed by what others expect of us at particular stages in our lives. Our false selves can become rigid and fail to adapt to our changing social roles. We then are threatened by change and may well cling to dogmatic beliefs and to the conviction that only we are right.

## 7. ISN'T IT PURE INSANITY TO KEEP GOING KNOWING YOU ARE HEADING IN THE WRONG DIRECTION? NO REGRETS, JUST START OVER. YOU CAN DO THIS. YOU HAVE LEARNED A LOT ALONG THE WAY, APPLY THAT KNOWLEDGE. BE BRAVE.

*You may have a fresh start any moment you choose, for this thing that we call 'failure' is not the falling down, but the staying down.*
### ~ MARY PICKFORD.

It has been said that it takes 21 days to form a new habit. 21 days out of an entire lifetime is like snapping your fingers. It is a short period of time relative to the many many years you have on earth. The next time you declare that your ideal goal is too hard to attain, try looking at it from this fresh new perspective. As you try new things or begin to form habits around the things that are working, know that the first, easiest path is to do what you can when you can. You can do it! Let go of old stories and renew your will by starting again; each week or each day and another day and another day... 21 days will be here before you know it.

Start fresh each week or each day by:

Working with your body, not against it. Dis-ease feeds on negativity, whether it's negative thoughts, actions or foods/drinks that the body cannot process. Setting your intention and then feeding yourself negativity in any form will put you back to square one. Accept, don't hate, what you have now. Appreciation for the magnificent form we call the body, no matter its present condition, helps decrease the chronic un-ease we call dis-ease.

Knowing that it takes steps to form a path. Wellness is a process of consistently making choices toward good health. If you stand in the same place complaining or not taking action, of course it will be impossible to see change. Feel encouraged by moving forward, even if you are doing one additional healthy activity a day.

Realizing that past disappointments can be celebrated; they help shape and refine your goals. OK, maybe you did not succeed with the last attempt. The best thing about "failing" is that you have a ready-made list of what doesn't work. You know not to try the same thing again right? Ask yourself how can you tweak what was done to get better results next time. Let go of the guilt and regret and understand that you are always learning.

Doing what you can when you are ready. Either you are ready for change or you are not. If you are ready, use that will to get through each day. Visualize what you want and hold those images in your mind. If you aren't ready for change, forcing yourself builds resistance and resentment to the activity, people around you and yourself.

Having fun! What do you have fun doing? Do you love to dance?

Enjoy singing when no one is around? Can't get enough of cleaning? Take what you love and infuse it in whatever healthy activity you are doing. Sing your favorite song while juicing. Dance all the way to your mat for situps. Smile for 5 minutes straight before meditation. Fun gives you fuel to keep going!

We are all meant to live happy, healthy lives.

## 8. NOT WHERE YOU WANT TO BE TODAY? KEEP GROWING, PROGRESS IS KEEPING YOU ALIVE. STOP GROWING, YOU'LL SLOWLY START DYING INSIDE. DON'T BE DISCOURAGED. YOU ARE TOO FAR AHEAD TO STOP NOW. FOCUS ON YOUR DESTINATION. BE PERSISTENT AND CONSISTENT. ONE AC-TION AFTER THE NEXT WILL LEAD YOU TO SUCCESS.

*Refuse to allow disappointment to develop as a result of things not working out the way you had imagined they would. God often takes you by a path that you have not known in order to get you to see something that you would not have seen.*

**~ MARSHA BURNS**

The race for success is a long one. Despite your zen-link aptitude at turning lemons into lemonade, life has a strange way of beating you down and stealing your dream.

It takes determination (and a lot of it) to keep moving forward in spite of the obstacles. Your legs get tired. You get thirsty. Every fiber of your being wants to just throw in the towel and call it quits. And yet your best chance at success (at winning the race) is in hanging on. In your determination to keep going.

If your entire life is practice and preparation for you being successful, then you spend most of your time working towards something that you might never get to realize until the very end.

It's the ultimate in deferred gratification. Which is hard for most of us.

How long do you keep trying after you stop enjoying what you're doing? The odds indicate that most of us will stop before we win the race.

So, if that's the case—that you have to go the distance—it's important to get serious about the race. The race is tough.

1. Stop thinking like it's a sprint. Prepare for the long haul.—Stay in shape mentally, physically, and financially. It's not about "getting rich quick" schemes or selfishly thinking only of yourself. Invest in your dream by thinking about the long effects of your activities. If it won't stand the test of time, don't do it.

2. You can recover from a few falls along the way. Don't get discouraged by failure.—You can't run and win the race at the same time. It doesn't make sense. You have to put in the effort to get back up from a few tumbles. You will get banged up. That's what happens. But you have to decide that the more you fall, the faster you get back up. No matter the damage, you will survive. Even from the bad stuff.

3. The finish line is hidden until you almost pass it. Keep pushing

forward without a guarantee about when you can stop.—Stop planning on getting a break any time soon. It's not worth what you'll give up when you do actually get to the finish line. Maybe you do get back in the race. Maybe you only give up temporarily. But maybe you don't. Maybe you become like everybody else around you who asks themselves, "What if?"... The key to being determined is not expecting to ever "catch a break".

4. Which next step isn't as important as you taking one? A long race is just a series of smaller steps.—Just do something. It's not about not making a bad decision. You can't avoid getting it wrong sometimes. You're human. You let emotion, passion, and will sway your ability to think like a computer. That's a good thing. Your illogic allows you to keep going long after it makes sense.

5. Everyone who's in the race with you is just as tired as you are. The difference is your ability to fight through the pain long after it stops being "fun".—If you're still in the race right now, take a look around. Those people around you are just as tired as you are. The pain you are feeling is the same pain that they have. It's no easier for anyone else. It's not harder for you. It's all about knowing you're hurting and deciding that you want success more than you want to avoid the pain.

There's not a lot to remember.

It's one foot in front of the other. You run as long as you can run. Then you walk until you can no longer walk. And then you crawl— pulling yourself by your fingertips until your knuckles cramp up. But you don't stop moving toward success.

You stay in the race and on your feet. Because the dream is something worth fighting for.

# 9. FEEL YOUR BLESSINGS JUST BECAUSE YOU WAKE UP THIS MORNING AND YOU'RE BREATHING AND HEALTHY. CONNECT WITH THE 'YOU' WITHIN. SAY IT LOUD THROUGHOUT THE DAY. I AM BLESSED. THANK YOU, THANK YOU, THANK YOU.

If you are struggling in your life and someone say's you should count your blessings, it sounds a little trite don't you think? But you see it is a sure-fire way to raise your energy vibration and attract good things into your life. Be grateful and get yourself out of the doldrums!

When we are feeling down and as though everything is against us, it is really hard to stay positive or visualize anything good, but this is what we need to do if we want change. While we stay down we are just going to attract more stuff to feel miserable about!

## Getting Rid Of the Negative Thoughts.

If we are angry, upset or hurt, negative thoughts will just keep rising, so acknowledge that you have these thoughts and then tell yourself that you are willing to let them go, punch a pillow or go for a run, get it out.

Now, it is no use trying to meditate or change our vibration while we are in this state, it just becomes a battle of wills and it won't work, it will only cause more frustration.

So this is where the counting your blessings comes in!

## Relax And Let Go.

We need to raise our vibration to get us out of the sticky angry mode, so instead of battling with it, we take our mind in a different direction.

Close your eyes and relax. Breathe deeply for a few minutes, and concentrate on your breathing, try to allow the tension to leave your body.

Now think of someone you love, see their face smiling at you, go through all the things that you love, tune into that feeling of love, really feel it.

Stay here and make sure you have thought of every good thing that you have or have experienced in your life and be grateful for it. Your vibration is now raised.

## We All Have Many Blessings.

When we feel love and gratitude, it is impossible for us to be negative, so make this a habit, to raise your energy level and lift you out of the negative state.

Think about everything you have in your life, from your home to food on the table!

Many people in this world have not had the opportunities that we have, but we take them for granted, when we take stock of what we actually have, we quickly realize that we are fortunate and blessed in many ways.

So make a blessings or gratitude list, and read it often, when you are in a positive state the Universe will bring you more things to be grateful for!

This exercise can do wonders and help anyone who is down and depressed about their life.

When we think of what we love and are grateful for our blessings, it is impossible to be down and negative, find your joy, count your blessings and let the Universe bless you with more! Learn to manifest love, joy and happiness.

My Success to you, to all you deserve and desire!

# 10. YOU CANNOT CONTROL THE EVENTS IN YOUR LIFE BUT YOU CAN CONTROL HOW TO REACT ABOUT THEM. BE SOLUTION FOCUS THAN PROBLEM ORIENTED. MAKE A CHOICE THAT WILL EMPOWER YOU INSTEAD OF ONE THAT WILL KEEP YOU IN A STATE OF A VICTIM. YOU ARE IN CHARGE OF YOUR LIFE.

What does it take to take charge of your life? When does it make sense to make the kind of changes that taking charge of your life implies? When you want to take charge of your life, you have questions you need to answer.

## Courage and Confidence.

It takes courage and confidence to take charge of your life. You might not feel an abundance in these areas right now if you're looking at taking charge of your life. Yet you have been courageous and confident during previous times in your life. Life requires courage! Life demands confidence!

Courage enables you to consider what might be a better set of choices. Courage gives you the get up and go to pick yourself up and take action. Courage does not replace fear. Instead, courage allows you to go forward despite fear that might be suggesting that it's too risky to move in the direction of your dreams.

Confidence allows you to use your talents and abilities in new ways. Confidence puts your skills to work in different circumstances. Confidence does not remove doubt. Rather, confidence allows you to do what you know how to do. Regardless of the doubt you may be feeling. In spite of reminders that today's circumstances are not precisely identical to how you've used your skills in the past.

## Change.

Change is inevitable. Life is filled with changes. Over the course of your lifetime, you'll live in an environment that presents many things to you, sometimes overwhelming you with the sense that your entire life is filled with change. As you face challenges and deal with change, it makes sense to adapt to the new situations that arise.

Taking charge of your life has to do with adjusting to the change as it occurs. Dramatic sudden change can leave your mind spinning. That's one time when taking charge of your life demands that you reach for all the courage and confidence you can muster.

## Skills.

You'll need to learn new skills. Times of change instill new skills. You can decide that you're willing to use your courage and confidence to gain the skills you need.

In fact, deciding is taking charge of your life. Because that makes it happen. I've found that when I reach deep for courage and confidence, I can decide to take action. I take charge of my life! I find that leads to happiness.

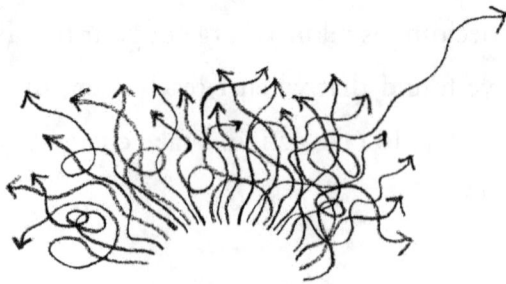

## CHAPTER 3

# KNOW THYSELF

*"The secret to joyful health for the mind, body,*

*and spirit is mindful living."*

**~ COACH PEGGY NELSON**

**Y**OU CANNOT MAKE great exploits or make use of all your potentials unless you understand who you truly are. Knowing yourself goes beyond understanding your nature or abilities, it extends to who you are with your inner mind.

## 1. YOUR ENEMY IS WITHIN. WORRY AND FRUSTRATION WILL NOT TAKE YOU TO THE NEXT LEVEL. DO SOMETHING TO FIND YOUR INNER PEACE AND JOY. STOP PRETENDING,

# BE ON A QUEST TO HEAL FROM WITHIN. IT'S IMPORTANT.

Many of us have by now heard the terms "living in the present" or "living in the now" or "living mindfully" or something along those lines. To some they're merely catch phrases of our time that have become socially popular. To others they're crazy ideas that aren't taken seriously. And to others (those who are fortunate enough to have been enlightened about and by them), they represent a new and higher level of understanding of life that if put into practice offers a new, positive, and transformative way of living.

In order to be the best person that you can possibly be, you must be able to maintain a state of peace and joy within yourself. Let's face it, if you are living your life in a state of turmoil and discouragement you are not operating at your highest capabilities nor are you experiencing your best possible life now. Here are three basic but powerful steps that you can apply in your life now in order to achieve an inner state of peace and joy regardless of outside circumstances. The three steps are 1) Make a Decision 2) Let Go and 3) Be Positive

The first step in achieving inner peace and joy is to decide that regardless of outside circumstances, you are going to maintain inner peace and joy. When you make the decision not to be moved by outside circumstances, you are taking control over your mental state of being. Even when you are confronted with challenges, such as a change in a relationship, getting behind on your bills, transferring careers etc. you have to remain unmovable in your decision not to let your circumstance effect your inner peace and joy. The way that you are going to remain unmovable in turbulent times is by finding something positive to focus on and something to be thankful for. When you consistently express gratitude, it takes your mind off of what you do not want and places your focus on more of what you do want. The expression of gratitude will wipe away your despair and give you the peaceful state of mind that you will need in order to move forward and overcome your challenges.

The second step in maintaining inner peace and joy is to choose to let go of all negative emotions that you have attached to people, places and things. Letting go is a major player in maintaining inner peace and joy. The following exercise will explain. The first thing I want you to do is to spend a couple of minutes focusing on something that you really enjoy. While you are focusing on what you enjoy pay close attention to your emotional response. Were you smiling? The second thing I want you to do is spend a couple of minutes focusing on something that you are not fond of. Again, notice your emotional response when you focus on what you are not fond of. Were you frowning? The point is, you will experience a negative or positive emotional response based on if your perception of a person or event is negative or positive. If you want to maintain inner peace and joy you must let go of all negative emotions and focus on things that bring you joy and give you peace.

The third step in maintaining inner peace and joy is to choose to live your life with a positive attitude by focusing only on the highest and best in everything. Remember that you will have an emotional response based on your perception of your experiences as being positive or negative. When you stay focused on seeing the best and highest in all people you are inviting joy and peace in your life because you are only seeing the good. When you see only the good, you are going to smile. Along with having a positive attitude you are also going to choose to make right choices. The right choice for maintaining inner peace and joy is to choose to respond positively when confronted with adverse situations that occurs in your life verses reacting negatively. When you take time and hold back from reacting negatively to an adverse situation and spend time considering the best possible solution before you respond, you are taking control of maintaining your state of inner peace and joy.

Maintaining inner peace and joy is a choice and when you practice focusing only on the positive in life you are making a choice to take control over inner peace and joy in your life. I received an email today about a man who was blind and because of unfortunate events that had occurred in his life it was necessary for him to move into a retirement home. During orientation one of the facility nurses described to the man what his room looked like. The blind man listened patiently and when the nurse finished speaking, the man stated that he was going to love his room. The nurse could not comprehend how the blind man could love the room when he had not even entered his room. The blind man stated that he made a choice long before arriving to the facility that he was going to love the room regardless. Friends, in order to maintain your inner peace and joy, you have to be like the blind man and wake up every morning with the mindset that you are going to live your life to the fullest in peace and with joy, regardless of whatever is going on in the world around you. Remember inner peace and joy is a choice.

## 2. JUST FOCUS ON THE NEXT STEP. DO NOT GET OVER-WHELMED ABOUT YOUR END RESULT, OR YOUR DESTINA-TION. IT WILL HAPPEN WITH ONLY ONE STEP AT A TIME. ONLY KNOW WHERE YOU ARE GOING AND WHY AND YOUR HOW WILL FOLLOW. JUST STEP UP. YOU WILL GET THERE.

When in the throes of the road to your dreams or goals it is easy to begin to let go or believe that you will never make it when all the results that you want are yet to appear.

People who begin going to the gym and after two weeks are yet to see their chiseled abs show up are prone to begin to start saying 'I'm done with this!' If only they would begin to look at the smaller results that were showing up then they would be able to continue on their road in a spirit of determination and faith.

If they were to ask the questions 'do I feel better?' 'do I have more energy?' 'am I eating better foods for me and liking them?' and found the answers to these in the positive then they would begin to see that they are actually making progress.

Though I've pointed to a persons' physical health the same can be said when working toward any other type of goal.

If for example it is your goal to make a certain product and market it then it is more than likely that at the start finding even an idea for a product may be eluding you.

At this point it is easy to fall into the trap of saying 'I'll never make it' but then you have forgotten the small triumph you've already had which is that you have already started looking for an idea for a product that you are going to make. This means that if you continue on your road then you will find it and to be frank the product is only the first step.

Even after it's done you will face the challenge of how to market it. After beginning to market it you will still have to persevere between when you've started marketing it and when the sales come in. Thereafter it will be a question of how to expand and whether or not to make more products in the same vein.

As you can see there will always be challenges along the way but the most important thing is to take it one step at a time. To face every challenge in a spirit of determination and when you best even the smallest hurdle to take stock of the triumph which you have had.

Though it may be tedious in the beginning making a small list of the things which you have achieved will help in showing you that you are indeed being successful. Always take stock of even the smallest bits of success in a journal, notebook or some other convenient place and you will begin to feel that the road is in fact leading somewhere.

Remember you could literally walk across a continent but the only way to do it is step by step.

## 3. TODAY YOU NEED TO MAKE A DECISION. YOU EITHER CONTINUE TO GROW OR STAY WHERE YOU ARE. ONE OF THOSE WILL LEAD YOU TO SUCCESS THE OTHER WILL KEEP YOU FEEDING YOUR FEARS. ARE YOU REALLY GOING TO SETTLE FOR LESS AND LESS UNTIL THE END AND CONTINUE

# TO LIVE YOUR REGRETS? TAKE OUT OF YOUR VOCABULARY TODAY...IF, COULD, WILL, CAN'T. NO MORE EXCUSES.

You only achieve what you set out for and you only get those results that you expect from yourself. What separates the successful people from the rest is what they expect from themselves. It is true that human mind is very powerful, what you conceive in your mind and what you believe will eventually turn to reality. If you think of yourself as mediocre result producing then you will only be able to produce mediocre results

Why you should never settle for less than you deserve is a good reason to refuse to live an ordinary existence. Your dreams transform into a belief in yourself and your abilities. It is a journey of ever constant evolution toward the goals in your life. Suddenly, the impossible develops into the possible.

But why do people choose to give in instead of struggling to get better opportunities? What about your life? Are you ready to keep going when things get hard? Or do you settle down for less?

So many people settle for ordinary in many aspects of their lives on a daily basis. They accept jobs they hate, deal with friends who let them down and let their relatives get away with wrongdoings. And if they do settle in life, it is because much too often, fear paralyzes and holds them back.

Furthermore, people suffer tremendous amounts of self-doubt. They are unable to believe they are good enough. There are always better options out there, but so many people have low self-esteem, which prevents them from understanding they can get better.

*"When it's obvious that the goal cannot be reached, don't*

*adjust the goals, adjust the action steps."*

**~ CONFUCIUS**

## When Reality Gets in Your Way.

Those words are maybe the best piece of advice you are ever going to get. Write them down. Burn or tattoo them onto your soul. Once you set a goal and decided in your life that you want to make come true, do not settle for less or let anything stop you from reaching it.

And yes, as you go forward, the reality is going to get in your way. There will be an inevitable slew of obstacles coming at you. But when it gets hard and you think that the path you take is not going to lead you where you want to go; do not abandon.

Rather than giving up on what you said you were going to do, find a different path. And you have to make that the cornerstone of your identity, in refusing to settle for less, bend or be broken by challenges or obstacles.

## Never Settle or Change Your Goal.

So instead, you rise to those challenges, doing whatever you have to, and devising any plan to find a way through it. Once that becomes your reaction, your life will change. Do not change what you believe in or your dream, but simply find another path in your creativity or some-one who can help you.

You have to do whatever it takes to get on the other side of it and build the life you want to see. But if your reaction is to change your goal, to make it easier by settling for less than whom you can be, you never are going to have something worth having.

*"The way you conquer self-doubt is by doing things that make you uncomfortable."*

**~ JESSE I.**

## Fear the Biggest Enemy.

But what is it that stops someone? The reason most people adjust their goals, settle for less, lower the bar or make it easier is because they are afraid. They are scared of what it says about them, thinking they cannot accomplish it, and even fearful of dreaming big.

And yes, most people are terrified of change, failure and even taking risks. This is one of the main reasons many of them settle for less in life. Yet, it is not about improbable goals or realization. It is about changing the things you can to be happy, not simply drifting along in life and complaining.

So, it is far easier to settle for less than it is to get out of your comfort zone. You can create endless excuses to justify the reasons but it results in you looking back with regret. Then, with a somewhat bruised ego, wishing you did not settle. But you must believe that inside, you have what it takes to persevere.

## If You Settle You Lose.

When something seems impossible, do not change it to something possible but rather find another way around it. There is always a path to make it or no one would have discovered anything in this world. Anyone, even you, can overcome things that were impossible yesterday.

As the generations pass, the level of patience is declining. People lack willpower and sadly make the mistake of picking the first option offered to them. It also applies to dreams, goals, and desires such as getting on a new career path. Things worth having take a lot of time and effort, which most people do not want to work for.

And although something may not be what someone really wants, it is often acceptable and becomes a habit. It then gets more comfortable to sustain that routine than to challenge oneself. Yet, you have to fight through all the obstacles that lie between where you are and where you want to be.

## How to Never Settle for Less.

Therefore, the minute you settle for less than you deserve, you get even less than you settled for. In general, people are lazy. They do not want to make too much of an effort, even if they are unhappy with their current situation. So, they lack the necessary willpower, self-belief, confidence, and ambition to make it.

And many times, people are so frustrated in life. They feel that settling for less will help them create the happiness they want. Yet, people constantly complain about their current situations, but do nothing to change it. Only the ones who are crazy enough to think they can; do.

So, ordinary or average is a place where you often get stuck not knowing how to escape. It is only by changing to a growth mindset instead of keeping a fixed one. In order to change, you must think differently, get rid of what is not working, learn from people with such mindset, create a plan of action and set that strategy in motion.

## Why You Should Never Settle.

And so, that is the key to accomplishment. The difference between the possible and the impossible is to understand that you should never settle for less. So believe you can get good at anything you set your mind to. Life is way too short to settle for anything less than what you truly want.

Therefore, the only way to reach your potential is to stop settling. You become your thoughts, so stop putting limits on yourself and do not waste your precious time. The moment you begin to settle in the most important roles of your life is the moment you begin to die a slow death.

So make that the pillar upon which all of your identity stands. And when times get hard, just go harder and never settle for less. Once you have the attitude that you deserve the best in life, you begin to get what you want, go places, meet people and wonderful things will come your way.

# 4. ARE YOU LETTING FEARS AND DISEASES MANAGE YOUR LIFE? ARE YOU HOLDING ON TO PAIN AND FEELING STUCK? THE POWER YOU NEED IS WITHIN. START BUILDING A LIFE INSIDE OUT, THIS IS THE FOUNDATION FOR A HAPPY LIFE. BE WILLING TO LEARN TO MASTER YOUR EMOTIONS ON A

## DAILY BASIS TO GROW. YOUR YESTERDAY IS GONE LAST NIGHT, IT DOES NOT MISS YOU. MOVE ON.

The things that we need could be nearer than we think. When we look for external things to bring us satisfaction, it may be found that true satisfaction never comes. Why is it that satisfaction does not seem to come from external things? Could that be because we already have everything that we need within us?

Take a look around you right now. Do you like what you see? Are you happy with your life?

If you aren't happy there could be a million reasons why. But those reasons will all have one thing in common. They all stem from YOU.

You might be surprised to learn this is the case. After all, if you are out of a job and you are struggling to get another one, is that necessarily your fault? If you never seem to have the money to get anywhere in life, is that your fault?

The truth is that every single situation you have ever gotten into in life has come as a result of YOU making decisions. If you think negatively you will get negative results, i.e. you don't think you will get that job so you don't try your best and you don't get it. But if you think positively, you will get positive results. You walk into the interview room for a job with the intention of showing them you are the best candidate for the job. Even if you don't get that specific job, how long do you think it will be before you land one with such a strong and positive attitude?

**All your powers lie within you.**

If you want to change your life and the situation around you, you need to understand that all changes come from within. Let's say you suddenly decide you don't like the wallpaper in your bedroom. You change it by choosing new wallpaper you like better, you buy it and you hang it. You look at your bedroom and you see that it's changed—but that change has come about as a result of thinking about how you can change it. Even though the change is external, it has still come from you.

This is the same kind of thinking that can drive every other change you want to make in your life. This applies to big changes as well as small ones. You may encounter obstacles *en route,* but the process of positive thinking holds true in every single situation. It always comes from within. If you know you can change, you can work towards making the desired changes happen.

**How good does your future look?**

You can probably see now that your future can look much brighter once you focus on the right way of thinking. It might help to make a list of all the things you want to change in your life right now, so you can get started on making those changes happen.

It can be overwhelming looking at a list like this, but think of it as the first major step towards changing your life for the better. Once you get the ball rolling and you become more familiar with using the power of positive thinking in your life, you will start to see changes occurring. You really can change your life from within—all you need to do is to get started.

## 5. ARE YOU HAPPY WITH WHAT YOU HAVE ACCOMPLISHED SO FAR IN YOUR LIFE? DO YOU KNOW WHAT WILL TAKE YOU TO THE NEXT LEVEL BUT FEARS HAVE BEEN KEEPING YOU HERE? ARE YOU DREAMING OF GOING FURTHER? THEN MAKE A DECISION TO LET GO OF YOUR FEARS TODAY. STEP INTO THE UNKNOWN TO MOVE CLOSER TO YOUR DESTINATION. COMMIT TO ONE ACTION TODAY THAT WILL LEAD YOU TO FULFILLMENT. JUST START. MIND TIME NOW, IT'S NOT PERMANENT.

Having a goal is the first step towards achieving it. But there are people whose lives are so constrained, that they have forgotten HOW to dream. Do you allow yourself the time, or energy to IMAGINE what you want to do with your life? If you have no desire to even contemplate the "what if's", this is one of the definitions of "depression". You are stuck in a pattern, but not even looking for a way out!

Do you wake up each day out of your bed without a clue where you're headed in life? Is a typical day waking up, going to classes, going back home to get something to eat, driving to work, coming home, sleeping, and repeat? Most people go through lives on autopilot, not knowing where they are headed.

What this means is that you need to know where you are going in life. This doesn't mean a physical destination, but rather what it is that you are working for every single day of your life. Why are you going to school besides the reason your parents put you there? Why are you going to work besides the reason to pay rent? Why are you stuck in a relationship that perhaps you don't like?

At any age, you get to choose your destiny. Even when you are at a point where you think to yourself that this is it, this is life, you can still go somewhere, become something else, and achieve what it is that you want. But you have to first be conscious of it, rather than let every day pass you by with no meaning. Here are some questions to play with if you are already unaware of where you want to go in life.

## Are you aiming for money?

Do you wish to live in a big house in Malibu next to the ocean driving a nice car such as a Mercedes-Benz? Do you want to buy diamonds for your lover as well as for yourself? Can you picture yourself going to Paris and sailing on a boat through one its rivers? How about traveling to around Asia trying out different types of exotic cuisines? Money is not only something that secures us, but brings unique pleasures that allow us to do what it is that we've always want to do in life, but never really got a chance to, and this is something that is worth aiming for.

## Are you aiming for family reasons?

Do you want to start a family and be a good dad or mom? Do you want to become a better parent to your kids than your parents were to you? Do you want to teach your kids to grow up and give them an opportunity that was better than yours? Starting a family with a loving spouse and children might be the thing that drives happiness to most people—

something that is an definitely admirable goal for someone to have.

## Are you aiming for personal growth?

Do you want to become better at a skill, perhaps a musical instrument? Do you want to be a better conversationalist with other people? Do you want to conquer fear and learn to live with excitement, with joy, and with happiness? Do you want to teach others what you have learned so far from your experiences and your wisdom? Personal growth is usually happens with years and years of discovering oneself, of not knowing who they really are inside, and then one day finding the things in life that makes him or her happy as well as becoming more in sync with oneself through the mind and body.

## Are you aiming for the meaning of life?

Perhaps you have achieved the things from above or similar gains, but it still has not fulfilled you. You want to learn more. You want to learn why it is that you were put on this earth? You want to be able to see yourself in the future looking back and actually say you were truly happy, that you have had a fulfilled life and there is not another thing that would like to do to make it better, and to understand that there is something beyond human beings, beyond just physical life itself, something that goes deeper beyond human understand but makes complete sense to you in the end.

## Why all this?

Figuring out where you want to go in like gives you a sense of right direction. You are not just waking up day after day doing the same thing with no ambition, no goal, and no purpose to fill your life with meaning and a sense of achievement. People who know what they want and where they want to go are proactive. They wake up every day with energy and clarity to get things done. People who don't know what they want or don't know where they want to go accept life as it as it is, do little to change their position, and grumble when they wake up.

## 6. HOW COMMITTED ARE YOU TO YOUR DREAMS? YOUR RE-SULTS DEPEND ON YOUR LEVEL OF COMMITMENT. YOU CANNOT EXPECT GREATNESS WHERE YOU ARE HALF COM-MITTED. IT IS TIME TO STOP BLAMING YOUR CIRCUM-STANCES. TAKE ACTION TO GET RESULTS AND YOU WILL BE GOING TO THE NEXT LEVEL. STOP SAYING YOUR OLD STO-RIES TO JUSTIFY YOUR LACK OF FULFILLMENT. FOCUS ON YOUR DESTINATION YOU ARE NOT THERE YET.

So much time and effort have been devoted to the significance that our dreams have on our personal achievements, and acquisition of our most essential goals. However, with that in mind, doesn't it seem somewhat perplexing that, while so many speak of their dreams (and how important they are to them), so little consideration is given, and action taken to actually CHASE them in a meaningful and impactful manner? Ideally, our most essential dreams drive us forward towards developing a person's vision that motivates us to create essential goals, that transforms us towards creating and using a personally worthwhile and transformable action plan.

1. This process requires that we first create a clear concept of what is most essential to us. It necessitates commencing with a sense of co-operation and coordination. When this is our mindset, we truly care passionately about our dreams and permits us to best cope with what-ever may necessitate additional focus and attention, in order to achieve our priorities and objectives. Chasing our dreams means consistently being clever in our approaches and pursuits.

2. Our primary objectives must be to prioritize doing whatever will best help those most significant and meaningful situations and scenar-ios. This only occurs when we avoid the far too easy path of blame and accusation, and consistently stress healing whatever wounds that will inevitably develop.

3. How can anyone pursue his dreams if he doesn't earnestly pos-sess an attitude that makes him stronger and drives him forward? One must articulate his aims, both to others, as well as (and more im-portantly) to himself, so as to use positive self—talk in a forward pro-pelling manner, that drives him to persist and persevere.

4. Are your expressed dreams actually your own, or are you simply expressing those you believe others will accept and will make you com-fortable? Only when they serve your personal needs and priorities, make sense (in the manner that they are realistically achievable, with the right degree of effort), and are service—oriented (to the betterment of others, as well as achieving what you deem most essential), will you truly pursue those dreams!

5. If those dreams are really significant to you, you have to enjoy what you are doing, and strive to establish an enduring methodology

that serves enhancing your focus and motivation. Focus on what you hold most dear and important, rather than merely trying to endear others.

Don't just dream or talk about them! Rather, do something meaningful about it.

What are the two necessary components in achieving your dreams?

## Believe.

Always believe in yourself even if the road ahead is tough. Expect resistance to happen each time you think of advancing. All worthy endeavors and causes in the past had met ridicule, negativism, and envy. Yours will not be spared.

Many well-known people—Walt Disney, Mark Victor Hansen, Oprah Winfrey, and Larry King—faced setbacks in their quest for phenomenal success.

Despite countless roadblocks, don't be discouraged. Focus on taking the first step... and the next. The more difficult the process is, the more you have to love yourself. Feed your brain with optimistic thoughts and nurture your dream regardless of the early outcomes.

If you're serious about success, remove the word "I can't" in your vocabulary. In fact, you have to practice a can-do attitude all the time. Always say "I can" regardless of the difficulty and result.

For every dream, there's a matching negativism that will cloud it. For every good intention and deed, there's an associated struggle and conflict. Be prepared and never give up.

A negative result only means a temporary setback rather than a failure. Learn from the mistakes that led to disappointments.

## Embrace change.

What are you willing to change to chase success? What behaviors and attitudes do you want to eliminate so you can achieve your dreams? What are you willing to give up so you can attain intense focus?

If you want success, change is unavoidable. A worthy cause can't be achieved without change. No change, no progress!

Stop all forms of negative energy. Who are some of your friends and family members that shower you with harmful comments and wrong advice? What thoughts make you feel hopeless and pessimistic? What endeavors and actions give you misery? What decisions have caused more troubles and heartaches than joy and fulfillment? What types of relationships hamper you from achieving success?

Identify unhelpful, problematic parts of your life and embrace change.

Change negative to positive force without delay. Discover the promise of a transformed life. Strengthen your self-image so others will respect you. Have a success mind-set even if the situation looks dim. Be willing to chase a productive lifestyle and your daily habits should lead to lifelong desires.

Since there are many wonderful ideas around, be open to possibilities. Let your mind absorb at least one profound idea daily and explore its potential. Don't discount an idea simply because it sounds impossible. Test it. Think about it. Give impossibility a chance to travel the road of possibility.

Believe in yourself and embrace change to improve your chance of reaching your dreams. But above all, believe that you have a divine assignment to accomplish. Our purpose is not simply existence but living life to the fullest.

## 7. WITHIN ALL OF US THERE IS A CONSTANT ARGUMENT BETWEEN THE LITTLE PERSON ARGUING THE PERSON THAT WANT TO GROW TO BE BIGGER AND WISER, STRONGER, RICHER AND SO ON. WE OFTEN A VICTIM OF OUR OWN. WE LET THE LITTLE PERSON WIN BECAUSE WE ARE NOT CONSISTENT AND DISCIPLINE ENOUGH. ARE YOU WILLING TO GO AND CONFRONT THIS LITTLE PERSON TODAY AND PICK UP WHERE YOU LEFT OFF AND WIN THAT BATTLE? DECIDE, COMMIT AND TAKE ACTION NOW OR YOU WILL LIVE WITH REGRET FOR THE REST OF YOUR LIFE.

Life can become a movie sometimes where we are the ones sitting back and watching life pass us by. We have many ideas to make our lives better but we seem to be stuck in an inertia phase.

You must take action now moving towards your goals or the outcomes in life that you wish to achieve. Psychologists have done a lot of research and have found many people are waiting until tomorrow or until something happens to them to start working on their goals. Many people unconsciously think someone will show up at your door, ring the bell, and then tell you, now have permission to get started working on your life and your goals. This is not the way it works; this is only a fantasy in your head. You must do the work yourself and you must get started now.

If you don't take action, you will regret it, whatever it is you need to take action for. You are someone who is filled with the get up and go to change your life in so many fantastic ways if only you would get up and do something about it.

Here are ways you can get up and take action:

## Wipe the slate clean.

If you have too many things on the go, clear them all and start from scratch. When you have wiped the slate clean, concentrate on thing at a time until it's finished and then move onto the next. If you can't clear everything, just drop them temporarily, concentrate on one thing until it's finished and then move on.

Prioritize—Pick the most important thing you have to do for the day, or week or year, and then pick the next most important thing and so on until you have reached the bottom off your list.

Eliminate distraction—Eliminate the things you do from day to day that distracts you from taking action for example TV, books, computer. When you eliminate distractions, your mind wants something to do and this makes you more inclined to take action on the things you want or need to do.

Take a day off—Maybe a bit contradictory this one. It's a simple piece of advice but one that is hard to do. Just take a whole day off, the world will still turn, the work will get done and nobody will die because you are not there. You will come back refreshed and ready to take action again which means you will be a lot more productive than you would have been should you have kept going.

Analysis paralysis—This is the term given to people who are analyzing things too much and it keeps them from moving on. Stop analyzing and just do it. There comes a time when you have to stop evaluating something and just bite the bullet and do it, if it doesn't work out do something else and start again.

## 8. YOU DID NOT HAVE DOMINION OVER YOUR PAST, LIFE WAS HAPPENING TO YOU. YOU SAID IT MANY TIME AND YOU WISH YOU COULD GO BACK AND CHANGE A LOT OF THINGS RIGHT? YOU KNOW BETTER NOW THAT COMPLAINT WILL NOT CHANGE YOUR PAST. WHAT ARE YOU DOING TO MANAGE YOUR NOW? THIS IS THE MOST PRECIOUS MOMENT OF YOUR LIFE, END THE CYCLE OF GUILT AND BLAME TO LIVE A FULFIL LIFE.

For many of us, guilt is like a certain kind of old friend—someone whom we willingly let in the door, and then can't kick out. Guilt shows up when we act in a way that doesn't sync with our goals and values—whether procrastinating, or breaking a promise, or taking credit for someone else's work. At its best, guilt acts like a moral compass, prompting us to reflect on what we're doing (or not doing), and then make constructive change.

But when guilt settles in for the long haul, serving up daily helpings of blame and shame without adding anything constructive to the mix, we find ourselves living with a parasite. Guilt shadows the good things in our lives. It whittles down our energy and self-worth. That's when we begin cheating ourselves of our personal dreams and needs. We make a habit of putting ourselves second, feeding our guilt, and starving our self-esteem—making it harder and harder to be our fullest, brightest, most creative selves.

Healing requires you to take a step back from all the complexity of the world, the variances of form, the differences and the divisions, the opinions of this doctor versus that doctor, the medications and their side effects, and focus on some basic healing principles instead. Forget about how difficult healing seems to be according to the world's dictates; the world knows little of healing.

## Breaking the Guilt Cycle.

The end of guilt is the end of sickness. Like all things about awakening, releasing guilt is a simple process. This is so because guilt always requires you to focus on the past, and the past is gone. It no longer exists at all, except in the mind of those who actively choose to focus on it, and by doing so force the past to remain with them.

Ending guilt asks only that you accept what is right now, and stop forcing your mind to dredge up and continually relive old wounds, pains, and regrets. Forget the past; it is gone and is therefore unreal. Healing can only occur by aligning with Reality, which is located in the present.

## Clinging to the Past Keeps Healing Away.

It is only your own clinging to old thoughts, dead ideas, and painful errors that keeps your past alive and real for you. Karma is but a belief fostered by the ego that you can never be free of the past, or that your release must be postponed until a magical future point arrives that is as equally imaginary as the past itself is. As with the past, there is no future! Only the present is real, or ever will be real.

Do not cling to the past, nor the future, but come to understand the passage of time for what it really is—a liberating force, not a prison house, from which you need no release, for the now is eternal and always present. So too is it with the body. You have no need to be freed from either one, nor does the karma that so many believe bind them to lifetimes of meditation and service in order to be undone.

## Change Your "Self-Image".

The purpose of this step is really one of transition. Its function is to make the journey easier and more gentle by gradually reducing fear along the way. It does not ask you to abandon your sense of ego altogether, which can, and often does, increase resistance and fear. It only asks that you allow the image you hold of yourself to progressively change from a negative-based perception to one grounded in gentleness.

How long this process takes is more in your own hands than you may realize. The sooner you accept a version of yourself that in no way conflicts with the gentleness and unconditional love inherent in your Self, with no exceptions, the sooner your conflict will be over. More and more, everything you do and think must come to reflect your highest Self.

# 9. DO YOU KNOW THAT WORRY SUPPRESSES YOUR IMMUNE SYSTEM? WHICH IS A BIG CAUSE OF YOU TAKING YOUR PILL DAILY AND YOU HAVE NOT GOTTEN THE BENEFIT OF TAKING IT. DON'T CONTINUE TO BE A VICTIM OF YOUR PAST NEGATIVE MEMORIES, AND OR RELATIONSHIPS. STOP BLAMING PEOPLE AROUND YOU. TAKE FULL RESPONSIBILITY FOR THE DECISIONS THAT LEAD YOU TO YOUR SITUATIONS AND MAKE A NEW CHOICE. RENEW YOURSELF TO START BEING HAPPY WITH WHO YOU'RE SEEING INSIDE

Just like a loaf of bread that's been left out too long, life can sometimes seem stale if we let routine take over. We get comfortable with what is and ignore what could be. Being present is important—it's the foundation of Power Living and experiencing the special moments in life. However, actively claiming your future is key to growth. Balancing the two modes is the trick.

When we think of renewal we often think of rebirth; something old dies and something new is born. By allowing our lives to mimic the cycles of nature we are reminded that no matter what happens to us there are always opportunities to shift a situation, to optimize our chances, and/or to start all over.

Whether you're looking for a complete overhaul or simply a fresh outlook, here are the ways to renew your life today:

**Streamline Your Life**—Although not a new concept by any stretch of the imagination, it's a concept that has been recently re-energized and re-imagined in the popular movement of "decluttering" your life.

**Begin something new**—Explore your creativity. Go back to

school. Learn a new language. Learn how to play an instrument. Be the stand-up comic or diva you always dreamed of being. Take better care of yourself. Create an inventory of your health including diet, exercise, genetics, and stress level. Begin slowly, one small change at a time. This is not about making a resolution every year to do better but rather a practical, soulful look at yourself and your health so that the years ahead can be lived to your fullest capacity.

**Start a Practice**—A new discipline will ensure that you invite mindfulness into your life. A daily practice affords you a timeout from your everyday routine. This is a gift to yourself; a commitment and promise to honor who you are.

**Be in Nature**—The outside world connects us to the cycle of life and the meaning of the seasons. Sometimes, when the world is still and Nature is dormant we need to be quiet and still as well. When the world comes back to life we are reminded that what has been still and quiet within us is ready to germinate and grow again. The cycle of life is the best reminder that nothing stays still, that life is always in constant flux, and that change is the norm.

# 10. YOU SURE HAVE TO KNOW WHERE YOU'RE HEADING TO END SOMEWHERE THAT YOU DESIRE. YOU CANNOT START DRIVING UNTIL YOU KNOW WHERE YOU'RE GOING. START YOUR DAY, WEEK, MONTH, YEAR WITH THE SAME ATTITUDE TO GET SOME RESULTS. WAKE WITH A DESTINATION AND A MINDSET TO GET WHERE YOU WANT. STOP LETTING YOUR DAY, WEEK, MONTH GUIDE YOU TO THE WRONG PATH

## AND COMPLAINT ABOUT IT. MAKE A COMMITMENT TO STOP THE CYCLE OF BLAMING AND GUILT. YOUR ATTITUDE DETERMINES YOUR END RESULTS. SHOOT FOR THE MOON YOU MIGHT CATCH SOME STARS IF MISSING YOUR TARGET. SET YOUR DESTINATION BEFORE YOU MAKE YOUR FIRST MOVE.

Consistently doing what you need to do to succeed, with total focus and resolve, is incredibly difficult. And that's why the ability to work hard and respond positively to failure and adversity is so crucial. Resolve, commitment, and determination help successful people work hard and stick to their long-term goals.

We all have something that we want. It could be professional, emotional, physical or spiritual in nature. To attain it, some effort is required, if the goal is ambitious, then a lot of effort is required. To achieve lofty goals, we need to have a combination of commitment and determination. Commitment is the act of binding yourself to a course of action. It is the motivation to assert ourselves even if there is opposition or there are obstacles in our path. Determination is our ability to try our best to keep on doing something even if it is very challenging to do so. Both of these qualities are required if you want to achieve a major change in your life. However, they require constant energy to maintain them. If you don't keep them up, you run the risk of not achieving your goals.

Your path to success is always based on the determination that you have engrained within yourself. Determination aligns your energy and attention towards your focus.

Determination is not whether you're a good or bad person, it's about what you're willing to do to achieve your end goal. Here are some of the best ways on how to be determined.

## Make the decision to be determined.

A strong, specific decision needs to be made so as to become more determined in anything. This decision indicates your direction. It shows you how to move forward even when you begin to encounter challenges on your path. This decision is set in stone, motivates you through hard times and keeps you focused during easy times. As such, determination begins by deciding what you want and sticking to your decision no matter what.

## Discover your 'why'.

Commitment is fueled by emotion. It is a motivation to keep going. For you to keep it burning, you need to have a strong why behind it. This is your reason for doing what you have chosen to pursue. Ensure that your why is strong. This will help you to know what to do next.

## Do not fear.

One of the biggest killers of determination is fear. When you are determined, you perform at a high level. However, fear interferes with this process and makes you deliver lower results than is required. As such, you have to be brave and face your fears so as to become more determined.

Let your past inform your future—and nothing more.

The past is valuable. Learn from your mistakes. Learn from the mistakes of others.

## Then let it go.

Easier said than done? It depends on your perspective. When something bad happens to you, see it as an opportunity to learn something you didn't know. When another person makes a mistake, don't just learn from it—see it as an opportunity to be kind, forgiving, and understanding.

The past is just training; it doesn't define you. Think about what went wrong but only in terms of how you will make sure that next time, you and the people around you will know how to make sure it goes right.

## Become deeply committed.

Being committed means to make a solid, well thought out plan that displays the best path to achieve your goals....and then sticking to it without deviating from your plan.

That's difficult enough but if you want to become great at what you do, you have to over-commit. Instead of running 5 miles, run 6 miles. Instead of watching TV, watch other masterful boxers display their craft. You have to make your entire life revolve around your desire.

## Narrow your choices.

Failure to strike out your distractions and detractors leads to a dimmed focus and soon you'll be unable to decide what to do, even though you know what's best for you.

On the other hand, if you identify what distracts you and stay committed to avoiding it, then you'll become much more focused on your goal.

Your mind will have fewer choices to make it wander around and come up with excuses for not taking a fight or going to train.

## Don't forget the finish line.

There's a well-known saying by Mike Tyson—"Everybody has a plan until they get punched in the face". This is when reality sinks in and you have to deal with the present situation.

There's no doubt there are times when nothing goes according to plan and you just feel like giving up.

These times are the most crucial points in your life and the decision you make will affect you for the rest of your life.

Fortitude is what will ultimately make you as a person and is what all great people are capable of, no matter how bad the situation is.

Don't forget, at times like this, the finish line is only within arm's reach.

## CHAPTER 4

# LIFE IS A GIFT

LIFE IS A GIFT and it offers us the chance, privilege, opportunity and responsibility to give something back by becoming more. Make 'your' today better than yesterday!

## 1. ONCE AGAIN TODAY YOU HAVE BEEN GIVEN ANOTHER OPPORTUNITY TO MAKE A BETTER CHOICE. TO BE A BETTER VERSION OF YOURSELF AND TO GROW FROM WITHIN. TAKE IT. GO FOR WHAT YOU WANT, BELIEVE IN YOUR POTENTIAL. REMOVE ALL BARRIERS AND LIMITATIONS FROM YOUR MIND AND JUMP HIGHER. STAY AHEAD AND DO NOT LOOK

# BACK. LIVE FROM INSIDE OUT IN THE PRESENT. NO ONE CAN BELIEVE IN YOU IF YOU DON'T BELIEVE IN YOURSELF. YOU HAVE ONE LIFE TO LIVE.

What do you believe about yourself? It is remarkably easy to become convinced of your limitations. Frequently, people discuss what they would love to have or do but "can't" for one reason or another. In some cases, there are huge challenges to overcome; however, all too often, what we perceive to be a physical, economical, physiological, or social boundary ends up being a mental boundary.

Extraordinary success requires emotional competence, mental clarity and a willingness to disrupt the status quo. You must release low-level thinking that holds you back. To be a standout, you must cultivate your strengths and work through fear and doubt to manifest your ideas. Emotional competence and mental clarity come from using those two warriors, time and patience, to your advantage.

## Emotional management.

To be successful, invest in your internal growth and personal development. You have to be your own best manager. When mistakes happen deal with the emotional consequences. Mistakes are the first steps in learning what has to change within you to achieve emotional balance and self-management. The better your self-knowledge, the more successful you will be.

Fear makes can prompt you to act too soon. Balance is when you can manage your impulse to please or be cutting.

## Have a purpose.

To be successful you need a purpose you will, without a shadow of a doubt, follow through to closure. A strong mission provides the motivation and unwavering belief required to be a standout success story. When you are clear about why you are investing your blood, sweat, tears, time and energy there is no room for laziness or complacency.

Time and patience keep you in touch with your commitment to succeed at all costs. Giving yourself time clears your mind and keeps you more tightly grounded to your overall purpose. It prevents you from being an impulsive decision maker.

Time and patience supply your deep will to pull-it-from-where-you- don't-have-it to stay the course no matter how hard things get or what challenges you face. You have to believe deeply that building your business is your opportunity to greatly change or influence the world.

## Renew yourself.

It is easy to be passionate when you are starting out, but successful entrepreneurs commit to keeping their energy levels high when they hit the inevitable, frustrating roadblocks. To be successful you have to care for yourself physically, emotionally, mentally and spiritually.

It is also important not to take things too seriously. That weakens your own emotional reserves. You have to bring a revitalized sense of renewed life into your business daily.

Your brain needs quality sleep, good nutrition and physical exercise to manage your thoughts and emotions at high levels. You have to keep your energy up. Taking time-out is crucial to staying fresh.

### Walk your talk.

You can talk about what you want to do so much that you develop an imaginary belief you have actually achieved your dream. To live your commitments you must understand that "trying" is unmoved energy. It is a form of the fatalistic thinking pattern of "potential."

If you don't know how to do what you want to do, then take the time to learn more, but at the end of the day you are the dependent variable in making something happen or not. Remember, there is no such thing as being totally "ready." There is always risk, so you must commit and put yourself in a situation where you have to make it work.

### Remain curious.

Curiosity is a form of innocence and a protection from fear. Curiosity gives you the courage to start a business that will breach status quo, possibly creating disruption. To find the courage to follow you curiosity about breaking boundaries, worries of consequences are placed to the side. Passionate curiosity is stronger than the fears of disruption.

The "what if" state-of-mind has a natural energetic drive that helps you to take risks you normally would not. Oftentimes, the more we are told "no" the more curious we become to see what would happen if we did it anyway.

## 2. STAY FOCUS ON YOUR STRENGTHS BECAUSE MOST PEOPLE AROUND YOU ONLY SEE YOUR WEAKNESSES. A LOT OF THEM SET THE BAR SO LOW FOR YOU, YOU MAKE NO EFFORT TO GO TO THE NEXT LEVEL. COMFORT IS USUALLY

# SYNONYM OF LACK OF FULFILLMENT. THERE IS A TIGER INSIDE OF YOU THAT IS READY TO SET FREE, THERE IS A HERO READY TO DO GREAT THINGS WITH YOUR LIFE. DON'T LET YOUR NUMBNESS CLOUD YOUR MIND. HAVE THE COURAGE TO TAKE A STAND FOR YOUR LIFE. MASTER YOUR LIFE. STOP WASTING YOUR TIME. YOU ARE POWERFUL, START BELIEVING IN YOU.

To do well in life, you must believe in yourself. You are the one person you can truly rely on. Your belief about yourself, and your abilities, reflects in your personal success and happiness. When you lack confidence in yourself, others pick up on that, and don't take you seriously, and in turn your confidence can shrink even more.

When it comes to success, nothing is more important and influential than self-confidence and belief in oneself. In fact, if we want to be successful, self-belief is more important than intelligence, talent, background, or just about anything else. In addition to this, people who have self-confidence and believe in themselves are healthier, happier, have better relationships, and are more motivated and resilient.

So what does it mean to believe in oneself and possess self-confidence? Loosely defined, it is the feeling of confidence in our judgment, abilities, and qualities. It is sometimes referred to as self-efficacy. This, in turn, affects almost every area of our lives, including how we think, feel and act. This is why it is so important.

All of us have made mistakes, experienced failure and felt disappointment in our lives. I know I certainly have had more than my fair share. Some of us have also been subjected to hardships and injustices.

All these experiences affect a person's self-confidence and faith in his or her own abilities. Fortunately, there are ways to develop a strong self-belief even though it does require some time and effort. It is important to remember that our past does not have to dictate our future. The only thing that matters is how we act today. So let's look at some empowering ways to build our confidence.

These are how to gain self-confidence and start believing in yourself:

## List your past successes and accomplishments.

Most of us are unduly hard on ourselves. We tend to recall our mistakes and failures more than our successes. Sure, we have fallen short and blundered as everyone has at one point. But we also have managed to overcome difficult situations successfully and accomplish things that we can be proud of. We tend to focus on our shortcomings rather than what we have achieved.

Make a list of all the things you have achieved in your life, both big and small. You will be surprised how many things you have accomplished that you overlook and do not give yourself credit for. Even more effective, add accomplishments to your list every day or every week and read it often. You are more capable than you realize.

## Seek positive feedback from others.

Ask the people closest to you to tell you about your positive traits, talents and skills. Since we tend to be extremely critical of ourselves, get positive feedback from others who are better able to see your virtues.

You may be surprised by what you hear and may learn that you have more going on for you than you realized. Positive reinforcement from others can be very powerful and empowering. The more regularly you do this, the bigger an impact is has on your self-confidence and belief.

## Build momentum.

When we act and take small steps, we start to build momentum. We know intuitively that once we start moving, our momentum makes it easier to keep going forward. This is why it is so important to take action, no matter how seemingly small. Much like a rocket launch that uses the most fuel in the first stage, once you start moving, your propulsion becomes easier.

## Think of a fear you have overcome.

When we lack confidence and self-belief, we become fearful that we are not good enough or worthy enough. We fear the consequences associated with failing so we do not try. This fear can be paralyzing as we all know. In order to counteract this fear, think of the times when you were scared of doing something but did it anyway and were successful. It could be the first time you dived into a pool, or when you asked someone out on a date, or the time you acted in a school play or played a musical instrument in front of a small audience. This might seem trivial, but write these instances down. We all have the ability to overcome fear. Very often, our minds exaggerate possible negative consequences and replay them over and over in our heads. Most of our fears are unwarranted. As Mark Twain said, "I have spent most of my life worrying about things that never happened".

## Celebrate the wins/give yourself credit

When you take small steps and accomplish small wins, celebrate them. If you walked for 5 minutes today, celebrate it and give yourself credit. If you successfully wrote 2 pages of your novel, celebrate it. If you ate 100 calories less today than you normally do, celebrate it. If you meditated for 3 minutes this morning, celebrate it. Focus on what you accomplished rather than what you did not. Keep a success journal and write in it every day. List the small victories you experienced and feel good about yourself. You deserve it. This is a very powerful habit that will help to change your mindset and give you confidence.

## Do your homework and prepare.

One way to overcome a lack of self-confidence is to prepare diligently. For example, let's say that you lack the confidence to give a speech. What will help bolster your confidence is doing your homework by researching your topic, practicing in front of a mirror, and rehearsing in front of a small number of trusted friends or family members who support you? All too often, when we lack the confidence that we can achieve something we want, we become paralyzed and do not even make the effort to prepare ourselves. Practice and preparation go a long way in helping you to build confidence in your abilities.

## Stop complaining.

Most of us know one or more negative people in our lives. These are the Negative Nancy's who find fault in and complain about nearly everything. When we complain, we are in essence highlighting things that are wrong instead of focusing on what is right. Pay attention to your mindset and stop complaining about circumstances because it only amplifies negativity and does not help your self-confidence. Speaking positively and optimistically helps to change our mindsets and provide us with the confidence that things will get better.

### Avoid negative people.

Just as we should surround ourselves with positive people who strengthen our self-confidence, we should avoid ones that do the opposite. Rid yourself of toxic friends, or at least limit the time you spend with them. Misery loves company so stay away from it.

# 3. MANY PEOPLE ARE LIVING BY OTHER PEOPLE STANDARDS. THEY ARE SETTING UP FOR LESS BECAUSE OTHERS MAKE THEM BELIEVE SO MANY LIMITATIONS. IF YOU ARE ONE OF THOSE, ONE DAY YOU WILL REALIZE YOU HAVE NEVER LIVE IN YOUR OWN TERMS. TODAY IT IS NOT TOO LATE TO MAKE A DIFFERENCE IN YOUR LIFE. TAKE CONTROL OF YOUR DESTINY. YOU DESERVE BETTER. GET OUT OF THE SHADOW AND START SHINING. TAKE FULL RESPONSIBILITY FOR YOURSELF. STEP OUTSIDE OF THE WORLDVIEW OF PEOPLE WHO DON'T SHARE YOUR VISION. SPEND TIME WITH YOUR INNER SELF.

Living life can be very challenging at times. Getting the hang of what works for you and what doesn't may take a very long time. Sometimes you get confused and frustrated by what you're doing, or where you're going. You may try to follow your own wisdom, but there are times when your internal navigational systems may throw you way off course. You may be lured away from where you need to be. Often, this siren's call comes in the form of well-intentioned people who may want to help you direct your life so that you do "the right thing." But people are not always so well-intentioned.

Sometimes, we trust other people more than ourselves, accepting another's opinions and views as more valid than our own. Somehow, we think they know what's better for us than we do—or we've been told that so often that we come to believe it. It's frequently the early influence of our family that sets this scenario in motion. Sometimes, confusion about who we are and what is best for us involves a deep-seated conflict focusing on allegiances to and boundaries with people who we deemed vitally important to our lives. Unchecked, this same familiar pattern may find its way into future relationships with spouses, bosses, mentors, or friends.

For some people, it's just simpler to allow others to keep doing for them what they need to learn to do for themselves. For others, there is a naive expectation that things will just come their way without having to take action on their own to make it happen. Still other times, there may be an unspoken agreement to sacrifice one's own authenticity in return for love.

The bottom line is that by not taking responsibility for ourselves, we too often allow others to take responsibility for us. And in doing this we are essentially giving them permission to take charge of our lives.

## It doesn't stop there.

There is an enormous price to pay for giving your life away in this way. It's simply not your life any longer; rather, it's someone else's projection of what your life should be. If this seems familiar to you, if you're passively drifting through life, barely participating in actively creating what happens to you, consider these suggestions:

## Take back ownership of yourself.

This is much easier said than done since this involves extricating yourself from a relationship where you've really been a passive participant. There may be a lot of protest and challenges from others who like things just the way they are and wish to keep the status quo. You may have to put up with this for a while before you learn to stand your ground. But before you can fully take your life back you may need to acknowledge regret for time lost. The only way to move forward is to acknowledge what has happened to you—how you got there, and what you need to do that's different from what you've done so far.

Although you may mourn the past and the fact that perhaps you should have taken charge of your own destiny years ago, it's essential to recognize, acknowledge, and accept that you have been responsible in part for the life you find yourself in, since you have not been fully present for yourself. You need to begin to identify and shift your attention to your own needs and goals. From a practical perspective, prioritize what's most important to you, regardless of what others think and feel about it.

Create a healthy space between yourself and your relationships.

Admittedly, this is a hard thing to do since so much of who we are as individuals is tied up with and dependent upon our most significant relationships. It's often difficult to be emotionally attached to someone while still remaining somewhat removed psychologically and intellectually. But creating enough room, a kind of "psychic space" between yourself and others, allows for enough personal expression while minimizing emotional and psychological entanglement. The goal is to gain a healthy perspective of others, without creating conflict within yourself.

## Recognize and acknowledge your own worth.

We all have specific abilities, talents, and skills but need validation, which at times we don't get from those we most want it from. When someone you count on for support refuses to acknowledge your positive qualities and abilities, it can undermine self-esteem and confidence. Beyond manipulative, this withholding behavior is often designed to keep a person dependent and needy. This is not someone who really cares about you.

## Heed the warning signs.

Watch out for individuals who don't have the time or inclination to work on the relationship they have with you—or on themselves, for that matter. Be wary of those who make you feel inadequate or "less than," or put you down, instead placing the burden on you to clean up your act so that the relationship can stay on course. Don't accept a relationship that is one-sided, limiting, and subtly undermining; where there is simply no room for you in the equation. Existing in an environment fraught with unhealthy undercurrents, threats both subtle and overt; jealousy; and one-sided conditions are potentially hazardous to your health and well-being.

**Don't try to fix people.**

Although "fixing" others may seem like a good idea it usually doesn't work because, from the other's perspective, there's nothing that needs to be fixed; there's nothing wrong with them—it's you that's the problem. Inevitably, these people will want not accept the fact that you've changed and will try to convince you to return to the way things once were. Don't do it. And if they continue along the same course, unable to accept who you've become apart from them, let them go.

# 4. WHAT WILL YOUR LIFE BE LIKE IF YOU DECIDE TO LET GO SOME OF YOUR FEARS AND TAKE A CHANCE TO ACT ON YOUR DREAMS? WHAT ARE THE BENEFITS OF NOT LIVING YOUR DREAMS? HAVE YOU BEEN CONVINCED THAT YOU'RE NOT GOOD ENOUGH TO GO ANY FURTHER IN LIFE? DON'T ALLOW YOUR INNER DOUBT CONVINCE YOU THAT YOU'RE NOT CAPABLE. YOUR POSSIBILITIES ARE LIMITLESS. START NURTURING YOUR HUNGER TO GET WHAT YOU WANT IN LIFE. STOP LIVING YOUR LIMITATIONS. ACT TODAY.

You are not born into this world to lack anything. There is enough to go around for everyone. It is up to each of you to collect how much you want using a spoon or a bucket. It's up to you to act or behave in accordance with your thinking of limitation or abundance. If your thinking is dominated by limitation, you are likely to believe it's not in your nature to enjoy the abundance of life and you willingly submit to an existence of scarcity, from which you adopt an attitude of lack and limitation.

We need to take a long, hard look at ourselves and recognize that we are capable of having whatever we want. We experience what we think of most of the time. If we mentally insist that we cannot have this or that due to some perceived reasons, we are likely to act to fulfil our limitations. Conversely, if we are absolutely convinced that we can change things for the better for ourselves, we create conditions that facilitate our actions to realize the desired outcome.

You can achieve almost anything in life. What you need is a great desire. The intensity of your desire determines your probability of achieving what you want. As the intensity of your desire increases so does your probability. Your burning desire coupled with your indomitable will to learn all that is required to achieve your goal makes any achievement inevitable.

Our limitations are never due to outside conditions. They always come from within us. To change our limitations, we need to identify the cause and deal directly and effectively with it. But most people try to change the external conditions and circumstances thinking they are the cause. This is a fruitless attempt. To remove the cause we have to look within us that is where it all happens. Change the cause and the desired effect automatically follows.

Once you realize that you cannot gain lasting happiness or satisfaction from achieving your potential from outside sources, the sooner you can become aware of the limitations of your external world. You then cease to seek remedy outside of yourself. You can begin to look inwards for all the solutions that you desire. It is always the inside-out approach that works. Dwell constantly on your limitations and they continue to reside in you.

Whatever your current circumstances are, there is always room for improvement. Believe strongly in yourself and your untapped potential. Realize that your true potential has not been fully developed. It is possible that you have as many qualities as, if not more than, other people who are more successful than you. Renounce your beliefs that you lack intelligence, education, wealth, fitness, health, good look, height, physical strength, social skill, etc. Ignore those who pass unfavorable comments regarding your appearance and abilities. Repeatedly replace your negative thoughts with positive ones until your mind is conditioned to think only positively. Being a positive thinker, you automatically banish from your mind all negative thoughts, and thus limitations.

Transforming your mind begins with changing the way you think. Acknowledge no limitations and there are none in your mind. Think great thoughts and remain great; think small thoughts and continue to be small. The choice is yours.

# 5. ARE YOU ONE OF THOSE PEOPLE WAITING FOR A MIRACLE TO HAPPEN? HOW LONG HAVE YOU BEEN WAITING? ARE YOU COMPLAINING NOTHING IS HAPPENING WHILE YOU'RE SEATING AND GETTING MORE AND MORE DISAPPOINTED? LET ME TELL YOU, THE ROAD YOU CHOOSE TODAY WILL DETERMINE YOUR FUTURE. YOU CANNOT REAP WHAT YOU NEVER SOW. GET MOVING, YOU ARE ALREADY RUNNING BEHIND, START GOING FOR WHAT YOU WANT. MAKE MIRACLES HAPPEN IN YOUR LIFE. DON'T SEAT THERE ANYMORE AND WAITING. NOTHING WILL HAPPEN WITHOUT ACTIONS FROM YOU. A STAR WITHIN YOU IS WAITING TO BE BORN.

One of the things that I realize is that sometimes we waste a lot of time on things that distract our attention from us working on our goals and dreams. Let me ask you a question. When working on a project, do you constantly have things getting in your way of what you really need to get done? What are those pesky distractions that always get in your way? Also, do you feel that you are wasting time in your life on things that are not positively contributing to your life? Are you ready to change the way you do things and get a lot more done in your day? If the answer is yes, here are the tips to get things done in your life:

Get a plan in place first thing in the day—Don't just go through your day, seize the day by having an awesome plan in place to keep yourself laser-focused.

Stop checking social media and Email—Imagine the number of minutes or possibly hours we could save if we didn't constantly check social media. Handle social media in time blocks; at certain times in the day and you'll be efficiently utilizing your time in the day.

Eliminate activities that drain you—Stop wasting time on people and activities that drain all the positive energy out of you. Focus in on those things that contribute positively to your life.

Stop worrying about things you can't control—Focus in on only things that you can do in life. Put your efforts into positive actions moving ahead.

Eliminate your focus on negativity—What you put your focus to is where you put action to and if you are putting your time into worrying and on negative things, I guarantee you will not get anywhere.

Stop hanging around toxic people—As I always say, you are too blessed to be stressed and hanging around negative people is going to stop you from really living up to your full potential. Do what you can to eliminate or limit your time around these energy drainers.

Start taking action on things instead of hoping for things—Imagine all the time in our lives that we have wasted by over-thinking things. It's time to stop hesitating and take action on the things we want do!

Start putting yourself first (not last) by making yourself important—When are you going to realize that your self-care and happiness is of the utmost importance? Stop wasting time! You only have one life and it's time for you to take great care of yourself.

Stop focusing on what others are doing—Are you constantly comparing yourself to someone else? Stop wasting your energy competing with other people's lives. No one is perfect. The only person you should be competing with is yourself.

Learn to stop looking back to the past—Your focus should always be on the present and moving forward. You are not your past. So do yourself a favor… stop looking back!

## 6. ARE YOU FEELING FRUSTRATED, SAD, CONFUSED? DO YOU KNOW WHAT YOU WANT BUT YOU FEEL STUCK? ARE YOU WILLING TO DO ONE THING TO GET OUT OF YOUR HEAD? MAKE A FIRST MOVE TO TAKE SOME CONTROL OF YOUR EMOTIONS. THESE FEELINGS MAY FEEL PERMANENT BUT THEY ARE NOT. YOU HAVE THE POWER TO CHANGE YOUR THOUGHTS TO CONTROL YOUR FEELINGS. YOU'RE NOT WEAK AND POWERLESS. YOU ARE STRONG AND POWERFUL. YOU BECOME WHAT YOU THINK ABOUT. TAKE THIS OPPORTUNITY TO MAKE A POSITIVE CHANGE IN YOUR LIFE. CONVINCE YOURSELF THAT YOU'RE GREAT, BECAUSE YOU ARE.

You must have a clear aim in life. Usually, your aim is to be successful in life. If that is so, then you must exert your will to make great efforts to attain success. Every one of you is endowed with the faculty of will, by which you decide on an action and perform the action to gain what you strongly want or wish for. This means success is achievable to all of you if only you will apply your willpower which is about the same.

Success can only come from within you. What goes on around you cannot bring you success. If you feel your purpose in life is to enjoy success, you must create a success mentality within you in order to experience success outside of yourself. If financial independence is what you intend to achieve, you must first change your inner feeling and mindset to feel and think like a wealthy person or a millionaire on the outside. Once you have assumed the thinking of a wealthy person, you will have increased the probability of setting yourself up for a life of financial abundance. Even if you suffer occasional financial setback, your wealth will be restored.

Success for accomplishing anything is possible for you if you apply your willpower and have an intense enthusiasm that springs from within you. If other people are enthusiastic about your success but you lack the enthusiasm, how then can you be successful? Chances are you are not likely to be successful. Besides enthusiasm, you just have to develop inwardly an unwavering determination and the all-important positive attitude to produce the desired result.

Having a desire may not be enough. You will be more motivated if you have a burning desire for success, financial or whatever, if that's what you want. Recognize fully the real necessity to build and maintain more and better relationships with others which is of crucial importance to your success. All these qualities must be inherent in you. Whatever qualities other people have, they cannot make you a successful person.

Your desire is dependent on how badly you want something. The greater your desire for success, the greater are your probabilities of achieving it. Having a strong desire entails having the will, perseverance and resolve to stay the course. Quitting is not an option. It is this passionate and unstoppable spirit that sees you through as long as you stay focused on your goal. Nothing can stop you and your success is virtually assured.

You will experience more successes if you adhere to your previous actions that have brought you successes. From your successes you will have steadily evolved a set of principles that govern your life. You consistently act in accordance with your principles that will guide you to more successes. Any significant deviations from your principles due to complacency will be certain to bring about your downfall and your successes will not be repeated. Your success is not due to a pure accident but an outcome of your will to take actions.

If you find attainment of success so elusive that you blame it on your bad luck, fate, parents, authority, environment, friends or even your neighbors, be fully aware that blaming others will only perpetuate your lack of success. Instead of blaming others, convince yourself totally that your failure to succeed is due to your lack of willpower, enthusiasm or passion. People are deficient on the outside chiefly because they are deficient on the inside. This is just a matter of changing their habitual way of negative thinking.

If you maintain a defeatist mindset, you will give in to failure too readily. You cannot control what is outside of you but you have the will to exert complete control over your own mind. Change your mind from wishful thinking to positive thinking. Know what you want and focus your mind on getting it.

## 7. WAKE UP THIS MORNING WITH A NEW ATTITUDE. MAKE A DECISION TO BE MORE THAN AVERAGE. YES, YOU HAVE BEEN TOLD YOU ARE NOT GOOD ENOUGH, YOU CANNOT DO ANY BETTER. PEOPLE SAYINGS DO NOT DETERMINE YOUR DESTINY. DEVELOP YOUR TALENTS THAT WERE GIVEN AT

# BIRTH. NO MORE SELF-PITY. BREAK THE CHAIN OF MISERY. FREE YOUR SOUL. RENEW YOUR MIND. START YOUR TRANS-FORMATION TODAY. VICTORY IS YOURS.

Self-renewal is about transforming yourself. It gives you a fresh life with renewed strength. You become a new person feeling better and more able, more competent and more effective by your willingness to adopt innovative ideas or appropriate measures.

Self-renewal is part of the self-development process and is a daily affair. Just about anything constructive you do every day contributes to your personal development that is inclusive of self-renewal, from reading a good motivational book to doing aerobic exercise. What about simple activities like a stroll in the park or a brief chat with the neighbor over a cup of tea? They certainly make you feel good. Anything that helps you feel good adds to your development.

The sheer volume of information available and the activities that you can get yourselves engaged in are all out there. The answers and solutions to your life's problems are abundant. Know what you want, what you desire to renew yourself. Access them and utilize them. It can easily change your life for the better. Perhaps, you don't need so much or so many of them; one or two ideas can bring tremendous difference to your life.

Personal development and self-renewal must be carried out on a daily basis for it to be effective. With so much information and knowledge to draw on to help you, and as each day passes with no effort expended on your part to make use of them, you are forgoing valuable use of your time for your daily self-renewal. Your procrastination and failure to see the urgency or importance of self-renewal cannot benefit you in terms of personal efficiency, productivity and creativity.

Self-renewing activities include looking after your well-being. Physical fitness is important, so devote sufficient time to daily physical exercises such as jogging and a brisk walk every day. Pay daily attention to relaxation, introspection, meditation, yoga or like activities that require you to be alone in a quiet spot uninterrupted for the duration you wish to be alone.

You need to get out of your comfort zone, and explore and venture into something new. Be prepared to take risks and develop the courage to act despite the fear. And most importantly, reverse your past conditioning, break old, bad habits and develop new ones. Ultimately, if none of these is acted on, it will be easy to be filled with deep regret in the years ahead.

To make certain that you practice self-development daily, you require self-imposed discipline. Self-discipline if strictly enforced ensures you do what you have to do but do not feel like doing. Those unimportant activities can be delegated, in place of which you can engage yourselves in activities that will bring about the kind of changes that you want for your life.

# 8. DO YOU KNOW THAT YOUR NEGATIVE EMOTIONS ARE KILLING YOU? YES THEY ARE. THEY ARE KILLING YOUR DRIVE, YOUR SPIRIT. THEY KEEP YOU POOR, THEY DESTROY YOUR ACCOMPLISHMENTS. THEY MAKE YOU THEIR PRISONER. YOU HAVE BEEN A SLAVE OF YOUR OWN NEGATIVE

# FEELINGS, THEY TELL YOU HOW FAR YOU WILL GO IN LIFE, AND THEY ALSO TELL YOU HOW POWERLESS YOU ARE. NOW YOU KNOW. WHAT ARE YOU WILLING TO DO TO SET FREE? ARE YOU READY TO START FRESH AND REMOVE THESE LIMITATIONS THAT YOUR OWN NEGATIVE FEELINGS HAVE PUT ONTO YOU? TAKE CHARGE OF YOUR FEELINGS OR YOU WILL BE A VICTIM FOR LIFE OF YOUR OWN BAD THOUGHTS. FEEL BETTER TODAY, YOU CONTROL WHAT YOU FEEL. YOU ARE WHAT YOU FEEL.

What would you give to be free of those unpleasant negative emotions once and for all? No more anger, anxiety or depression. If you are like the majority of us, you would give a tremendous amount to escape their uncomfortable clutches.

The world widely perceives negative emotions as something to be 'rid of' or 'cured' and, ashamed of these emotions, no one really talks about them. In some instances, doctor's diagnose the 'condition' as a 'disorder' and prescribe medication for the 'defective brain'.

What if I told you that the answer to true freedom from negative emotions lies, not in expelling them from your life, but from embracing them with open arms?

The fact is that the more you resist an emotion the more powerful it becomes. Like an airtight plastic bottle, the more forcibly you push it down into the water, the more tenaciously it propels to the surface. Instead, if emotions are permitted to be felt, they do in fact transform on their own.

The word emotion is derived from the Latin *emovere*, which means to "move through or out.". So, as the definition would suggest, by allowing emotions to arise and naturally move through us as they wish, they will eventually pass out. It is by clinging, forcing and rejecting emotions that we disrupt the natural flow and we cause them to mutate into ferocious monsters.

We are human beings at the end of the day and feeling emotion is part of being alive. Making peace with all of the emotions that we feel, accepting them and allowing them, is the surest way to flow with life instead of against it.

Here are the things that you can do to free yourself from these negative emotions:

## Stop Justifying.

First and foremost, you need to stop justifying getting angry and upset over everything. Stop thinking that you're entitled to be so negative, because you're not. The only person responsible for this is you. Do you really want to become that cranky old man or woman that tells everyone they ever meet why everything is awful and why everyone sucks? You know who I'm talking about, you've seen them in the grocery line. If you stop justifying your negativity to yourself you won't have a reason to be angry, and much more people will actually enjoy being around you. Get over the spilt milk.

## Stop Making Excuses.

You need to stop making excuses for both yourself and others. Perhaps you rationalize your own actions and why it's okay for you to verbalize

your anger. Or maybe you create explanations as to why other people deserve your anger. Either way, you're trying to invent a socially acceptable explanation for your behavior. The only problem is that it probably isn't acceptable and all it's doing is keeping your negative emotions alive and making you miserable in the meantime. Eventually there will be no one left to care but yourself. Stop making yourself a victim. Really think about whether or not these other people have actually done anything wrong.

### Start Taking Responsibility.

Now that you've stopped making excuses, it's time to take some responsibility for yourself and your actions. As soon as you do this, you will start depriving your negative emotions of the power they hold over you. What right do they have to your life anyway? Own your problems and your actions and stop blaming other people. It's called being a happy, functional adult.

### Be Grateful.

Instead of constantly obsessing over how crap your life is, start being grateful. What are the things or people you have in your life that you can be thankful for? Start defining your life by the good, as opposed to the bad. Get into this habit by thinking of at least one thing every day that you're grateful for.

## 9. WHAT DO YOU WANT TO CHANGE? ARE YOU LIVING DISSATISFIED WITH NO PURPOSE? WHEN WAS THE LAST TIME

# YOU WERE PROUD OF YOURSELF? LOOK AROUND TODAY AND DECIDE TO HAVE A BETTER RELATIONSHIP WITH YOURSELF. LOVE YOURSELF NO MATTER WHAT. RELEASE FROM YOUR MIND ALL FEARS, ANXIETY, RESENTMENT, OR SUFFERING. YOU HAVE WHAT IT TAKES.

Can you honestly say that you love yourself? Are you having a hard time being happy with yourself? It is so easy to focus on your faults and everyone can dwell on their insecurities instead of the things about themselves that they are happy with. Doing this can cause you to dislike yourself. You may also be too busy focusing on others around you and not focusing on loving yourself. Some people don't want to be alone and fear to do things on their own. This can really hinder your journey to self-love, as you have to learn to be comfortable being with yourself.

## Why Is It So Important To Love Yourself?

This may seem more important to some than others, but self-love is one of the best things you can do for yourself.

Being in love with yourself provides you with self-confidence, self-worth and it will generally help you feel more positive. You may also find that it is easier for you to fall in love once you have learned to love yourself first.

If you can learn to love yourself, you will be much happier and will learn how to best take care of yourself. When you are truly in love with yourself and happy, you should stop comparing yourself to others so much and should find yourself more confident, not worrying as much about what others think.

Here is how to love yourself:

### Have Fun by Yourself.

It's always good to have a few days set by for yourself, that is just for you to do something fun. In doing this you can learn to enjoy your own company, and most likely feel more confident doing it on your own.

This could be, going to the cinema, going on a date with yourself or finding new things to try.

### Forgive Yourself For Your Mistakes.

Reflecting on your mistakes can help you to forgive and forget. If you can look back at some poor choices you may have made, and forgive yourself, you can start to move on and forget about the past. Loving yourself despite any mistakes you made in the past is great for your self-worth.

### Surprise Yourself.

Try things out of your control, and say yes to things you would not normally say yes to. This will also help you with getting to know yourself. You may find out that you enjoy things you never realized or tried before. Try and get out of your comfort zone and see what happens.

### Pursue New Interests.

It's great to try something new that you have wanted to try for a while, or have been too scared to do.

You never know what you might enjoy until you try it, so think of a new hobby you could try, or go to a place you've wanted to go to for a while.

### Give Yourself Credit Where Credit Is Due.

Celebrate your achievements! Just like when you list your accomplishments, it's good to actually celebrate your achievements. Tell others about what you have done, share your experience and be proud of what you have done. Give yourself the credit you deserve.

### Take Care of Yourself.

This one probably seems obvious, but taking care of yourself plays a big part in learning how to love yourself, and a lot of people do not it. If you take care of yourself, you will be the best version of yourself. Take a look at our self-care ideas to get you started.

# 10. WE ALL GET INFLUENCED IN COUNTLESS WAYS THAT TRIGGER WITHIN US SOME REACTIONS AND PUSH US TOWARD SOME ACTIONS. OFTEN, OUR ACTIONS AND BELIEFS ARE LIMITED BY OUR PERSPECTIVE. THE WAY WE PERCEIVE THE WORLD WILL SHAPE OUR INTERACTIONS AND THE CHOICES WE MAKE. BE OPENED TO OTHER'S PERSPECTIVE. BE LESS JUDGMENTAL. DON'T BE A PRISONER TO YOUR PAST MEMORIES AND EXPERIENCES. RECOGNIZE YOUR STRENGTHS AND LIMITING BELIEFS. CHALLENGE YOURSELF TO GREATNESS.

If a limitation is self-imposed, it is one that we have forced ourselves to accept and is not forced on us by somebody else. For example, our limitations which are the result of mistaken beliefs, wrong assumptions or false perceptions are self-imposed. As long as we do not accept them, no one can control our mind by imposing any forms of limitations on us.

Our limitations limit our thinking. But we need to think big if we want to succeed and be happy in life. There isn't a doubt about it. This cannot possibly happen if we accept self-imposed limitations blindly which result in serious character defects and personal failing.

If all our life we think small, we remain small. If we see ourselves as someone who can only run a small stall, then ever a small stall owner we will be. A personal prophecy is fulfilled. But is that a realistic image of our own selves? If we refuse to impose limit on our thinking, and give ourselves a chance, we could very well be managing a large self-owned business.

The complete removal of all self-imposed limitations is essential if we are seeking a way for self-improvement. Improvement is essential for us to emerge as a better and more successful person. We should not allow anything to hinder our efforts to accomplish positive change for ourselves. We deserve better things, and this is only possible if our mind is free from any limited thinking.

Our limited thinking dictates the way we act and behave. All the negative emotions such as fear, anger, hostility, annoyance, displeasure, etc. that we experience are the effects of our misperceptions and wrong beliefs. It's we who have decided by ourselves to be filled with them.

No external force forces them on us or influences us to own them. If we can just use a lot of our willpower not to internalize these emotions, we can be ever free from them.

To be able to handle our destructive emotions, especially fear and anger, we need to identify the causes that led us to become such emotional being. We should continue to be open-minded by willing to consider ideas and opinions that are new or different to our own. This means we must be prepared to challenge, disprove, question and test our flawed assumptions, incorrect perceptions and erroneous beliefs in the light of new evidence, incidents and personal experiences.

Some people are antisocial. It's not that they choose not to be sociable. They are self-conscious, especially when they are in a crowd. They have this self-imposed belief that they do not possess good looks or are not able to engage in a long and interesting face-to-face conversation, and so they conclude they are certain to suffer ridicule or rejection at a party. Their feeling of personal inadequacy and shyness prevent them from making their first attempt at attending such a gathering. Even if they attend a gathering they are likely to read it as rejection if the people there are just as shy and slow to respond. By believing that their opinions of themselves are the only correct ones, their lives are likely to become devoid of social activities. Usually, other people do not share their way of thinking.

Be aware of the vast potential that lies hidden in you. What is deeply disappointing is your failure to realize your vast potential which results in developing only a tiny part of what you are extremely capable of achieving. You lose out because your hopes or expectations have not been fulfilled. Cast away this instant your self-imposed limitations and set yourself completely free to finally find fulfilment of your lifelong dreams.

## Chapter 5

# FOLLOW YOUR DREAMS

THE BIGGEST ADVENTURE you can take is to live the life of your dreams. Stay focused, go after your dreams and keep moving towards your goals. Keep your dreams alive!

## 1. WAKE UP FEELING GRATEFUL JUST BECAUSE YOU ARE ALIVE. YOU ARE ONE OF THE LUCKY ONES. YOU HAVE BEEN CHOSEN AND BLESSED WITH INFINITE POTENTIAL. YOU ARE AMAZING. IF YOU DON'T BELIEVE ME, GO BACK AND THINK OF ALL YOUR ACHIEVEMENTS THUS FAR. AREN'T YOU AMAZING? HUH... IT IS NOT YOUR JOB TO FOCUS ON YOUR

# FLAWS. LET OTHERS DO THEIR JOB BECAUSE THEY ARE GOOD AT IT. START A POSITIVE CONVERSATION WITH YOURSELF. LIFE IS GOOD. START LIVING TODAY.

Self-realization is the act of understanding and fulfilling by your own efforts of your own potential and overcoming personal weaknesses that you have not been aware of. It involves rational and impartial observation of your own emotional and mental states, and recognizing the possibilities of personal development with regard to your ethical principle.

The sooner you attain your self-realization the better it will be for you that you are responsible for pursuing you own wishes, and not through some outside intervention. Whatever happened and will happen to you is your responsibility. The life of everyone is in their own hands. Your character, mental power, existence and well-being are exactly what you have intended them to be. Whether you gain happiness or satisfaction or otherwise is up to you to fully achieve your potential.

It is through self-realization that you develop self-reliance. Self-reliance does not come about through seeking the direct intervention of some supernatural being, especially through prayers. Therefore, all the things that you dream of, you put all your efforts into making them come true. You strive for and attain your ideals.

When you live up to your ideals, your character grows in strength and influence. You become an excellent example to emulate and an inspiration to others. Self-realization gives you the freedom to gain insight into the nature of things, and the emotional and mental states as evident in other people. It frees you from wrong perceptions, false beliefs and unacceptable behavior. You learn to realize that self-effort is the only way to solve all your personal problems. Others may lend a helping hand, but make self-dependency a personal habit of yours.

There are significant and serious weaknesses inherent in every one of us. It is only when we start the process of self-realization that we can uncover the awful state we are in—a state in which we are burdened with misperceptions, mistaken assumptions, invalid generalization, flawed biases, false beliefs, wrong views and more. It is these flaws of ours that give rise to our ignorance, anger and greed, and they can only be overcome through self-realization.

We are solely responsible for all that happen in our life. Our fortunes or misfortunes are not determined by some external influences. They are the results of our good or bad actions and deeds committed previously. People who continue indefinitely to carry out and commit harmful, illegal or immoral actions and other evil deeds without considering that they are liable to experience misfortunes in this world or perhaps in the next world have not reached self-realization. Blaming others for your misfortune is easy but laying the blame on others will not change your situations. Understand that you cannot escape from retribution for the sins of your past life. That is the natural law.

The laws of nature can be understood fully by anyone through constant practice of self-realization. Those who fail to acknowledge the existence of these laws tend not to have a moral conscience and are very likely to commit misdeeds. However, if you are concerned more with the needs of others than with your own, and render selfless service to others, your good deeds will mitigate your past sins.

## 2. ARE YOU HEADING TO THE RIGHT DIRECTION? 1, 2, 3...5 YEAR FROM NOW WILL YOU BE SATISFIED YOU MADE THIS CHOICE YOU ARE MAKING NOW? IF YOU ARE NOT SURE WHERE YOU ARE HEADING YOU WILL END UP WHERE YOU DON'T WANT TO. TAKE CONTROL OF YOUR DESTINATION. REGRET AFTER THESE YEARS WILL NOT TAKE YOU THERE. USE YOUR TALENTS. THIS IS THE DAY YOU DECIDE TO BE-COME MORE THAN AVERAGE. STOP THINKING ABOUT WHAT YOU CANNOT DO, BUT WHAT YOU ARE MADE TO DO AND WHAT YOU'RE GOOD AT. DON'T LET YOURSELF CONVINCE BY THE LITTLE VOICE IN YOUR HEAD YOU WILL NOT SUC-CEED. MAKE YOUR OWN CHOICE. YOU ARE GOOD ENOUGH.

Act "as if" You start off each day not always feeling the way you would like to. You may want to feel happy or cheerful but due to a reason or two, your feeling is not what you would like it to be. However, you can feel a particular feeling whenever and wherever you want to. You can act or behave as if you already have the feeling that you want. Your action will cause the feeling that is consistent with your desired feeling to arise within you. You can "fake it till you make it."

You can become an outstanding individual of integrity by consciously acting as if you are already one. If you behave like a person who has strong moral principles, your consistent behavior will create within you the habits of such a person. It becomes your reality.

Change yourself to change your life—If you want to change your life, you must change yourself. The change must come from within you if you want it to be enduring. If you want to lead a life of generosity and success, you must begin to develop within you the qualities of being generous and successful. You cannot perform kindly acts unless you are a kindly person. Change empowers you, and you gain happiness and satisfaction by fully achieving your potential

Personal change can only come to you when you realize you need to change. To know what to change, you need to acknowledge the existence of weaknesses within you and recognize what they are. You do that by identifying what is delaying or holding you back in terms of personal development or progress. Your weaknesses may run up a list which you feel you are committed to overcome.

Don't let vanity stand in your way to being a better person—Vanity is excessive pride in your own self. It is only human nature to want to take pride in your appearance, abilities and achievements. You want to have attractive appearance, exceptional abilities and be admired for your high achievements. Nothing's wrong with that. However, all of you have your respective shortcomings and faults. These are weaknesses in your character which you are almost never aware of.

Having all the desired appearance, abilities, and achievements that you have, are they enough to make you an outstanding individual? How could you if you cannot see yourself in the way other people see you. Usually, others know you more than you know yourself. Most of the times, you are in denial about your personal weaknesses. Any comments on them are met with angry argument from you.

Don't react to circumstances but create your own—We are responsible for the way we think. When we think, we create a state of mind which evokes the emotions that we feel. These emotions are either positive or negative, and they affect our circumstances. Unfortunately, most of us let circumstances dictate the way we think. If we are caught in a traffic jam, we react with anger. If someone passes a careless remark, we feel annoyed. That's the way we are. We react to circumstances all the time instead of creating them.

### The point is to get started.

You can acquire all the knowledge you wish to have. You can devise a ten-point action plan to improve yourself. But if you don't apply your knowledge or implement your plan, it is just as good as not having the knowledge or the plan. People generally have vast knowledge, ambitious plans or big dreams. But some are successful while others are not. What distinguishes the successful ones from those who are not successful is taking action.

### We can be masters of our own fate.

We all can be masters of our own fate. Every one of us must take responsibility for where we are and what we do in our lives. Those who lead unsuccessful lives find this hard to accept. All along we think other people are the causes that we find ourselves in this predicament. Or we blame situations outside of ourselves for our lack of success. This we believe justifies all the emotions from resentment to hatred that we feel towards others.

You must have a goal—If you don't have a destination, how do you know where you are going? If your life has no destination, you are like a raft cast adrift, floating on the sea and is not controlled by you.

This is the same as not having a clear purpose in life and not knowing what you want to do. Eventually, like the flotsam you are washed up on an unintended beach and get firmly stuck there for life.

Is that what you intend your life to be? You must have a goal in life—an expressed aim that your plans or actions are intended to achieve. Having a goal gives you a purpose and a course along which you must take to achieve that primary purpose. It provides a reason for your existence. If you don't have a goal, how do you know how much progress you have made towards accomplishing your task or how much you have succeeded in your life? Your goals are the only way to measure what you have done.

## 3. TAKE THE OPPORTUNITY TO REFLECT ON YOUR ACCOMPLISHMENTS. START MAKING SOME NEW PLANS. FOCUS ON YOUR SUCCESS AND BLESSINGS FOR THE YEAR. RENEW YOUR MIND AND SPIRIT. TODAY IS YOUR PRECIOUS GIFT. TAKE CARE OF YOURSELF AND MAKE SOME GREATER CHOICES. LEAVE BEHIND ALL REGRETS, DISAPPOINTMENT, AND GUILT TO MOVE ON FREE INTO THE NEXT STAGE OF YOUR LIFE.

Life can be dramatically different when you focus on your blessings instead of your shortcomings. In fact, the world has a brighter color when you think and talk about the aspects of your life that are working instead of the areas that are frustrating you.

Your living conditions and future are determined by what you do in the present moment. Your past and your future do not play a role in the determination. Your past is gone and your future is yet to arrive.

Your past has provided you with valuable lessons which you have learnt and made you a wiser person. Whatever happened in the past cannot be changed. Any regret you have about the past is of no use as the past remains unchangeable. Your worries about the future do not help also. What you worry about may not happen. Whenever you regret about the past or worry about the future, you place yourself out of the present moment.

It is the present that you should focus your mind on at all times. The present is all you have now. No matter what happens to your life, it is always at the present moment. You are living and enjoying your life, as well as suffering the pains in the present moment. You can only be creative in the present moment which is important to you as it is the only time you can use to plan and make decisions for the future.

How often have you allowed your mind to lose control in the present moment as it wanders to the past or future? You are not in control of your mind if you are constantly focusing on the past or future. Instead of having control over your mind, you allow it to control you. When that happens, you are not using your mind in a productive way as you can only be productive in the present moment.

If you can consistently focus your mind in the present moment, you will find you are entirely free from problems. Problems don't exist in the present moment. They exist only when your mind wanders to the future. All your problems are about the future. How much of your present moment have you spent waiting for the boat trip along the coast that you are going to take next summer or thinking of the job promotion that you are confident of getting or of your child reaching a certain age or of having the desired amount of savings? It is always about the future.

It's like you want to live in the future and don't want the present. You are not living, growing and developing. Bring your attention back to the present and you notice you start to live again. When you live in the present moment, you create for the future by whatever you do.

If you look forward to enjoying something in the future, you can't enjoy it now as the future is yet to arrive. Also, now is the only time that exists and when the anticipated enjoyment arrives, you will have it in the now, no longer the future.

## 4. YOU CANNOT WALK INTO A NEW YEAR WITH YOUR OLD MINDSET AND THINK EVERYTHING WILL BE BETTER. DO NOT FOOL YOURSELF. YOU CANNOT GAIN SELF-ACCEPTANCE, POSITIVITY, CONFIDENCE IF YOU STILL NEED APPROVAL OF OTHERS WITH THE SAME OLD ATTITUDE. START DOING WHAT YOU NEED TO DO TODAY TO IMPACT YOUR LIFE. BELIEVE IN YOURSELF, TAKE RESPONSIBILITY FOR YOUR ACTIONS THAT LEAD YOU TO MISERY AND MAKE SOME CHANGES. DON'T WALK INTO THE YEAR WITH YOUR OLD MASK AND THINKING THINGS WILL BE BETTER. TAKE CARE OF YOURSELF AND COMMIT TO BE YOUR BEST STEPPING INTO A NEW YEAR.

One of the best, unforeseen consequence of simplifying our lives is it has allowed us to begin living our lives in the present. Eliminating nonessential possessions has freed us from many of the emotions associated with past lives that were keeping us stuck. And clearing our home has allowed us the freedom to shape our lives today around our most important values.

## Why you should live in the present moment.

The problems with constantly running ahead of ourselves are numerous.

For a start, it leaves us disconnected from ourselves and from the present. We miss out on the exciting and beautiful things that are happening to and around us at this very moment; we miss the opportunity to connect deeply with others, to learn important life lessons. Your present may seem messy and stressful right now, but I guarantee it won't be any different further along the line unless you learn to overcome the challenges that face you now.

When you leave the responsibility of change to your future self in order to feel safe now, you are storing up more and more problems for you to deal with at a later date. So, as long as you avoid and skim around the truth that is facing you now, the more likely it is that you will find yourself in the exact same position further on down the line. In order for change to take place and to start living the life that you want, you have to start living for the today.

Choosing to live in the past or the future not only robs you of enjoyment today, it robs you of truly living. The only important moment is the present moment. With that goal in mind, consider these tips below to start living your life in the present:

Remove unneeded possessions—Minimalism forces you to live in the present. Removing items associated with past memories or lives frees us up to stop living in the past and start living in the present.

Smile—Each day is full of endless possibilities! Start it with a smile. You are in control of your attitude every morning, keep it optimistic and expectant.

Don't dwell on past accomplishments—If you are still talking about what you did yesterday, you haven't done much today.

Stop worrying—You can't fully appreciate today if you worry too much about tomorrow. Realize that tomorrow is going to happen whether you worry about it or not. And since worry has never accomplished anything for anybody, redirect your mental energy elsewhere.

Think beyond old solutions to problems—Our world is changing so fast that most of yesterday's solutions are no longer the right answers today. Don't get locked into a "but that's how we've always done it" mentality. Yesterday's solutions are not today's solutions and they are certainly not tomorrow's solutions.

Conquer addictions—Addictions in your life hold you hostage. They keep you from living a completely free life today. Find some help. Take the steps. And remove their influence over your life.

If you can only live one moment at a time, you might as well make it the present.

# 5. WHERE WOULD YOU BE IF OTHERS DID NOT INFLUENCED YOU NEGATIVELY SO BADLY? WHERE WOULD YOU BE IF YOU HAVE CONTROL OF YOUR EMOTIONS AND YOUR DESTINY?

# WHERE WILL YOU BE IF YOU STOP LISTENING THE SMALL VOICES IN YOUR HEAD? TODAY YOU HAVE A DECISION TO MAKE. YOU CANNOT EXPECT YOUR CONDITION TO CHANGE WITH YOUR OLD MINDSET. DON'T WALK AROUND EXPECTING MIRACLES TO HAPPEN. TURN YOUR LIFE INTO A MASTERPIECE BY MAKING MIRACLES IN YOUR LIFE. MAKE SURE YOUR ACTIONS TODAY ARE MOVING YOU IN THE DIRECTION OF WHAT YOU WANT. START BELIEVING IN YOURSELF.

When you have self-control you have the ability to exert control over your feelings and reactions, and to conduct yourself calmly and sensibly in difficult situations or when you are excited, angry, etc.

Self-control implies having the power to do the right things and refrain from doing the wrong things in life. In other words, focus entirely on the things you want and the things you want to do, and not to pay attention to those things that you don't want and don't want to do. But it requires strict discipline to do the things you have to do, and not to do the things you shouldn't do. Discipline—self-discipline—is an essential element in self-control.

Regularly practice calmness of mind and you are on the surest way to possessing self-control and attaining success. At the same time, eradicate those undesirable imperfections, and discard negative emotions in your character and develop those that are positive. You stand to gain tremendously and increasingly take control of your life. Cultivate the essential attribute of composure that has all along lain latent inside you and make maximum use of it. Composure is a rare quality and yours is likely to be much admired.

When you consistently practice self-control you are very unlikely to be unduly influenced by any emotions. You certainly gain much for yourself and emerge as a better person than many who lack the ability to their emotions or behavior. For example, you do not totally lose your composure and begin speaking out loudly, or become moody and easily irritated at any times. You do not use profanities which you know indicate a lack of self-control and self-respect. Your qualities are quickly noticed, praised and imitated. Those around you benefit directly from your emotional stability.

Self-control includes mind control. Control your mind or it controls you. There is no other alternative. Mind control requires strict discipline to be successful. An effective method of managing your mind is to keep your mind fully occupied in some ways. Proper mind control facilitates the attainment of goals, success, happiness, etc.

One effective way to develop self-control is self-conditioning. Constantly visualize yourself with absolute self-control and act on a daily or regular basis as if you already possess this quality until it becomes a habit of yours. Frequently use affirmations and self-talks. These methods are effective enough to produce the desired results. When you have mastered self-control, you constantly appear calm and relaxed for these are your natural state. People think you are lucky to be born with self-control but you know better—it is the well-deserved reward of your careful and persistent effort.

# 6. MOST PEOPLE OPERATE LIKE THEY HAVE NO SOUL. THEY ARE SO FOCUS IN WHAT IN FRONT OF THEM THEY LOSE ALL

THEIR IMAGINATION ABOUT WHAT THEY CAN CREATE. IF YOU HAVE SHUT DOWN YOUR IMAGINATION DUE TO STRESS AND FRUSTRATION OF LIFE, TODAY IS THE DAY TO TAKE THAT BACK. START LIVING WITH PASSION. THE MOST POWERFUL TOOL WITHIN YOU IS YOUR MIND. CONTROL YOUR THOUGHTS AND YOUR CIRCUMSTANCES WILL NOT BE THE SAME. YOU HAVE ALL WITHIN YOUR MIND TO GO AS FAR AS YOU WANT IN LIFE. REGAIN CONTROL OF YOUR MIND AND FIGHT YOUR DEVILS. WITHIN YOUR MIND YOU WILL FIND FREEDOM AND YOU WILL START CREATING THE LIFE YOU DESERVE. TAKE CONTROL NOW. NEW YEAR NEW MIND AND SUCCESS WILL FOLLOW. TAKE THE CHALLENGE.

Since we were born, our minds have been gradually programmed by our surroundings and by society at large. As we grow, evolve and awaken to this reality, we learn that it is in our best interests to uninstall some of this programming and take back control of our minds.

What are we taking control back from, specifically? Well, in part, the immense amount of cultural, societal and institutional brainwashing that has greatly influenced who we are and how we view ourselves and our abilities.

You can clear yourself of this corrupt thinking and reclaim your sanity and effectiveness. But it's hard, because distractions are everywhere, pulling at us and creating needless points of focus meant to disempower us. They drive us into compulsive consumerism and egotism, rather than meaningful connections and emotional freedom.

So today, it's time to flip the switch. It's time to free your mind and take back control of your life. Here are the smart ways to start doing just that:

## Prioritize your desires ahead of external and internal resistance.

You're the one that's got to die when it's time for you to die, so let yourself live life the way you want to live it. Seriously, life is too short to waste profuse amounts of time wondering what other people think about you. In the first place, if they had better things going on in their lives, they wouldn't have the time to sit around and talk about you. What should be important to you is not their opinions of you, but your opinion of yourself. So don't let others get in your way!

## Stop looking for and expecting "perfect."

You are flawed, so is everyone you know, and that's just as it should be. Seriously, have no fear of perfection; you will never reach it. And don't expect that others will achieve it either. We're all imperfect beings filled with flaws and imperfections, therefore we shouldn't wish to highlight the weaknesses of others at the expense of denying our own. In the end, you will come to realize that perfection, especially in relationships, is only ever found in the beauty and honest appreciation of imperfection.

## Give yourself a break.

Yes, you have battles out in the world to fight, insecurities to overcome, loved ones to contend with and goals to achieve, but a break from it all is necessary. It's perfectly healthy to pause and let the world spin without you for a while. If you don't, you will burn yourself out. So refill your bucket on a regular basis.

Loosen your grip on the past.—Sometimes we have to let go of what's killing us, even if it's killing us to let go. Letting go means to come to the realization that some circumstances and relationships are a part of your history, but not a part of your destiny. Cry. Forgive. Learn. Move forward. Let your tears water the seeds of your future happiness. And remember, sometimes the hardest part isn't the act of letting go but rather learning to start over. This is normal. This is a new day. A new beginning. And things will change for the better.

# 7. IF TODAY WAS THE LAST DAY OF THE YEAR, YOU HAVE BEEN GIVEN 365 DAYS TO TURN YOUR LIFE AROUND. WILL YOU BE SATISFIED WITH EVERYTHING YOU HAVE ACCOMPLISHED? IF NOT WHAT WILL BE THE FIRST THING YOU DO TO TAKE CONTROL OF YOUR DESTINY IN THE MORNING OF THE NEW YEAR? WILL IT BE ANOTHER YEAR OF DISAPPOINTMENT, STRESS, GUILT, LOW-SELF-ESTEEM, POWERLESSNESS, AND FEAR THAT YOU WILL BE CARRYING AROUND? MAKE A DECISION NOW. YOU MIGHT NOT HAVE THE SAME OPPORTUNITY. START YOUR YEAR COUNTING YOUR BLESSINGS, WITH DETERMINATION, STRENGTH, AND COURAGE. DEFY THE ODDS. LEAVE YOUR CIRCUMSTANCES BEHIND. NO MORE EXCUSES. WHAT IF THIS IS YOUR LAST YEAR? THEN MAKE IT YOUR BEST. TAKE WITH YOU TO THE

# NEW YEAR HAPPINESS, LOVE, COMPASSION, KINDNESS, WEALTH AND AN OPEN MIND.

Most people don't know the profound effects of making decisions. Often times, we go through life oblivious to what thoughts we are thinking and what actions we are taking. Every single decision we make in our days shapes our current reality. It shapes who we are as a person because we habitually follow through with the decisions we make without even realizing it.

If you choose to confront the options before you with courage and confidence, you open yourself to a fulfilling path of your own design, filled with numerous possibilities. Rather than procrastinate in fear of making the wrong decision, weigh your options and act on the best one—revel in the chance to create the life you want to live.

If you're unhappy with the results in your life right now, making the effort to changing your decisions starting today will be the key to creating the person you want to be and the life you want to have in the future. Let's talk about a few ways you can go about making life changing decisions.

### Realize the power of decision making.

Before you start making a decision, you have to understand what a decision does. Any decision that you make causes a chain of events to happen.

### Go with your gut.

Often times, we take too much time to make a decision because we're afraid of what's going to happen. As a result of this, we go through things like careful planning, deep analysis, and pros and cons before deciding. This is a very time consuming process. Instead, learn to trust your gut instinct. For the most part, your first instinct is usually the one that is correct or the one that you truly wanted to go with. Even if you end up making a mistake, going with your gut still makes you a more confident decision maker compared to someone who takes all day to decide.

## Carry your decision out.

When you make a decision, act on it. Commit to making a real decision. What's a real decision? It's when you decide on something, and that decision is carried out through action. It's pointless to make a decision and have it played out in your head, but not doing anything about it. That's the same as not making a decision at all. If you want to make real changes in life, you have to make it a habit to apply action with your decision until it's completed. By going through this so many times, you will feel more confident with accomplishing the next decision that you have in mind.

## Learn from your past decisions.

The truth is you are going to mess up at times when it comes to making decisions and instead of beating yourself up over it, learn something from it. Ask yourself, what was good about the decision I made? What was bad about it? What can I learn from it so I can make a better decision next time? Remember, don't put so much emphasis focusing on short term effects; instead focus on the long term effects.

Anything you decide to do from this point on can have a profound effect later on. Opportunities are always waiting for you. Examine the decisions that you currently have in the day. Are there any that can be changed to improve your life in some way? Are there any decisions that you can make today that can create a better tomorrow?

## 8. LET ME TELL YOU THE DREAMS YOU HAVE BEEN HOLDING ON TO CAN AND WILL COME THROUGH THIS YEAR IF YOU DECIDE TO LET GO OF YOUR FEARS. YOU HAVE BEEN GIVEN ANOTHER OPPORTUNITY TO LIVE A BETTER LIFE, TAKE IT. MAKE THE DECISION TO KEEP YOUR MIND SHARP FOCUSING ON YOUR PURPOSE. YOUR MINDSET WILL EITHER LEAD YOU OR DESTROY YOU. YOU HAVE THE POWER TO TRANSFORM YOUR LIFE. MAKE THIS YEAR ABOUT YOU. START STRONG BY MAKING BETTER CHOICES. LEAVE THE BLAMING GAME BEHIND. REPROGRAM YOUR MIND; CHANGE YOUR ENVIRONMENT IF IT NEEDS TO. DECIDE TO MOVE AROUND WITH LIFE TWISTS AND TURNS. DON'T LET YOUR NEGATIVE THOUGHTS HOLD YOU A PRISONER. TAKE CONTROL OF YOUR DESTINY.

Of all the negative emotions that can reduce your capacity for attracting what you desire, fear is one of the most potent. Are you anxious, stressed and frightened when you think about everything that could go wrong in life?

If so, you're not alone! However, you do need to develop a strategy for changing this mindset. Fear holds you back and keeps you focused on the idea of lack, while love fills you with positivity and heightens your energy vibration in a way that makes your manifestation abilities much more powerful. Here are things you can start doing immediately if you want to learn how to let go of your fears:

## Understand Your Fears.

First, you need to analyze your worries and find the root of your unhappiness. This isn't an easy process. It can be quite scary actually. Many prefer to just ignore their fears because they don't want to look deeper into them. But in order to become emotionally stronger, we need to address the problem, not hide from it.

## Embrace And Master Your Emotions.

It's important to understand that transforming fear into love isn't about repressing or denying the truth of your feeling. Mastering your emotions is a useful skill here; the thought is that you can fully embrace those emotions, acknowledge them, and find a way of processing them so they can be let go.

Write in a journal, get them out through creative pursuits (such as painting or playing music), or channel them into physical endeavors like running, horse riding, dancing or boxing.

## Write Down Your Fears.

This may seem counterintuitive as you will be focusing on your fears. But sometimes facing your problems is important in order to finally let them go. Find the courage to sit down and write down what has been worrying you.

You will see that some fears are actually ridiculous when put on paper and it will be easy for you to forget about them.

## Stay Open.

It's natural to shut down during times of fear, even if you're normally an open person. The next time you feel fear starting to undermine you, fight to keep your mind and heart open to possible courses of action.

Ask yourself what you can do to feel better in your current situation, take small but deliberate steps out of your comfort zone, and let other people care for you when they want to (instead of pushing them away). Don't isolate yourself or keep all your worries hidden; use your support network, and know there's no shame in making yourself vulnerable.

## Focus On Doing Good.

At the bottom, we all yearn to be heard, valued and truly seen by other people. Consequently, one of the most meaningful gestures you can make is just to sit with another person and lend a non-judgmental ear to whatever they want to say. Provide empathy, work to understand them, and be fully present in the moment.

# 9. START STRONG, FOCUS ON THE PRIZE. IF YOU HAVE NOT MADE YOUR CHOICES YET, YOU ARE STILL ON TIME. AS OF NOW YOU ARE ABLE TO MAKE A DIFFERENCE IN YOUR LIFE.

# YOUR LIFE IS WHAT YOU MAKE OF IT. NO MATTER HOW DIFFICULT IS YOUR CIRCUMSTANCE YOU HAVE A CHOICE TO MAKE, THE CHOICE MAY LEAD YOU TO HAPPINESS, SUCCESS OR DEPRESSION, HOPELESSNESS AND SO ON. THINK BEFORE YOU ACT. MIND YOUR LIFE.

It is true that our mind is very fickle. It keeps chattering all the time with or without our permission. It is also a fact that it does not listen to our will when we wish to focus it on anything. Even if we force our mind to do something; it, like a naughty boy, start playing its own game as soon as the force is relaxed.

When you make a decision to do or not to do something, and you use your self-discipline to stick resolutely to your decision even if you don't want to, you are also practicing self-control. You feel good inside and in control of your life. The more you discipline yourself, the more self-respect you develop. More self-respect increases your self-confidence and self-esteem.

Everyone likes to achieve something and be successful. But to achieve something does not come easy. Attaining an achievement usually involves thorough preparation, making considerable sacrifices, and more importantly supreme self-discipline. There is simply no alternative to accomplishing something with one's own effort, courage and a right dose of self-discipline.

## Discipline Your Body.

If you can discipline your body, your mind shall be disciplined. This is a time tested technique which is used by all military academies all over the world to discipline the mind of the soldiers. The training starts with the discipline of their body and soon their mind is so disciplined that they can jump from a cliff by an order of their boss. The same principle is behind Yoga, Meditation, rituals, fasting and numerous other methods which discipline the body and hence discipline the mind.

## Mind Your Emotion.

Many people wear their emotions on their sleeve. They fall in love every alternate day and then curse the other person for not responding to their gesture. They hate almost everyone and then wonder why others hate them so much.

You have to make yourself less vulnerable to emotional stress by limiting your dependence on only few people. You must also take care of the emotions of other people so that they also take care of your emotions. Once you are emotionally stable, your mind shall not waver.

## Strengthen Your Soul.

Someone has said wisely that if you win the world but lose your soul, it is of no value. You nurture your soul by doing righteous, moral and legal actions according to your conscience and for the benefit of all human beings. However, some people don't mind selling their soul for a dime. Once they lose their soul, the mind loses direction. Soul is like a light that directs our mind to the right direction. Without it, mind start ruling you and you become its servant. To keep your soul, develop faith in God or in Humanity. If your faith is intact, your mind has to follow your orders without questioning.

# 10. TODAY IS A DAY OF BLESSING AND GRACE. START STRONG. THIS IS YOUR MOMENT. TURN YOUR LIFE AROUND AND START LIVING LIKE YOU MEAN IT. MAKE BETTER CHOICES. LIVE FULLY AND DECIDE TO TAKE CONTROL OF YOUR DESTINY. FIND OUT WHAT YOU'RE MADE OF BY TAKING THE CHALLENGE TO START LIVING A MEANINGFUL LIFE. THE DIFFICULTIES YOU ARE GOING THROUGH ARE PART OF LIFE NOT YOUR LIFE. BE ALIVE.

It can be easy to run through the maze of life without pausing to think of its meaning.

Does what I'm doing matter?

More importantly, does it matter to me?

Feeling that what you're doing has a real purpose and meaning that matters to you can make a huge difference in your life. It makes getting up each day the most exciting thing in the world. You can't wait to get started. Forget trying to force yourself to work hard, it becomes more important to remind yourself to take breaks to eat!

We all want to live a meaningful life since after all, we only have one chance at doing this. Happiness and fulfillment is much more attractive than emptiness, which makes living a life with some kind of meaning one of the widest held goals in the world.

People measure their success in terms of meaningful actions. You will find that everyone is obsessed with life meaning—starting from philosophers and scientists to the ordinary man. And while there is no single or final answer to living a meaningful life, there are several things you can do to get closer to this goal.

## Focus on the Important Things.

We all have some things that are more important than others. Pinpointing this is something you must do on your own, since there is no general definition as to what's most important in your life.

Once you determine the top 5 things that you find to be essential to your happiness, use them to live the life as you want it. If you prioritize your family, focus on spending time with them. If you like singing, turn this into your hobby or job. In other words, pursue your passion in life. The world is your limit.

## Find Your Life's Purpose.

If someone put a gun to your head and said 'give me one reason for you to live', what would this reason be? What do you stand for? What is your life's purpose? If you want to make your life meaningful, you need to find its meaning first. Otherwise, you cannot really set a meaningful goal.

## Be Aware of Your Actions.

What can you improve or change? Review the actions you take on a regular basis to learn what made you stray from your goal or imagined path. Focusing on details will help you accomplish more, as long as you are prepared to make some changes.

## Find Some Courage.

You need to be courageous to live, but living a meaningful life requires a lot more courage. After all, you need to make many changes to achieve this, try new things and put yourself out there.

Once you determine the essential actions to improve your way of living, you can easily find courage. Don't be afraid to be different or try something new—you can rarely achieve your biggest goals without a bit of a risk.

## Focus.

Rather than micromanaging 20 goals and focusing your attention on them all, focus on one thing at a time. This does not mean that you will leave the rest of your priorities behind. It solely means that you will dedicate all your energy in making sure they are all achieved, step by step.

You can easily achieve this. Make a habit of creating a list of goals you will do over the day or the week, not further. This list should consist of things that are achievable and realistic to avoid failure. If you learn how to do things at their time, you can achieve more.

## Simplify the Life.

This may sound strange, but in order to make your living meaningful, you have to make the life simpler. The life is more meaningful if you spend your time doing things that fulfill you, so get rid of all those things that cause stress and frustration and basically, simplify your way of living.

# Chapter 6

# BE GRATEFUL

EVERY DAY is a new opportunity given to you be become a better person. Don't let your negative thoughts take over your mind. Find something to be grateful for every day, that'll be a powerful lesson to you.

## 1. DO YOU KEEP GOING BACK TO THE OLD VERSION OF YOURSELF BECAUSE OF FEARS? ARE YOU UNABLE TO MOVE ON BECAUSE YOU FEEL COMFORTABLE? TO LIVE YOUR DREAMS YOU NEED TO GET OUT OF YOUR COMFORT ZONE. PEOPLE ARE SOMETIMES CONDITIONED TO BE MISERABLE

# BECAUSE THAT'S WHY THEY KNOW BEST. IT'S TIME TO GET OUT OF YOUR HEAD TO FIND THE BEST 'YOU'. YOU DON'T OWE ANYTHING TO OTHERS TO STAY STRESSED, FRUSTRATED, AND DISAPPOINTED. MIND YOU, REACH HIGHER FOR THE SKY. BE YOUR OWN BOSS. START LIVING WITH PASSION AND ENERGY. MOVE ON FROM THE MINDSET THAT IS KEEPING YOUR SOUL AND SPIRIT POOR OF DESERVING JOY. STEP UP

Comfort zone is a situation in which you feel comfortable with your present level of average achievement or non-achievement. There is no real desire to move out of your comfort zone to overcome your inability to initiate or begin something new. As a result, your ability and determination are not being tested and you remain where you are for as long as you are not prepared to take risks.

People in comfort zone typically live a passive existence and refuse to accept responsibilities which involve risks, and having to be accountable. Living in the comfort zone is safer as you need not have to shoulder any responsibility. You move through life aimlessly or involuntarily waiting things to happen rather than taking action to cause change. Accepting responsibilities involves being self-reliant and taking risks.

Since there is no certainty of success in taking risks which involves moving out of your comfort zone, there is considerable reluctance among you to do anything as everything involves risks. However, you need not take unnecessary risks. By taking calculated risks, you are likely to be on course to overcome all your unpleasant emotions caused by the self-perceived threat of danger, pain or harm. Your unwillingness to do something can only change when something happens to you or you make a firm decision to change your personal situation. Something that happens to you must be big enough to jolt you out of your comfort zone. It has to shock you deeply in order to make you act or change, a good example of which is the loss of your job.

It's a harsh fact of life that you know your lives are not growing or developing, yet you refuse to change out of fears. Indeed, the greatest obstacle to your personal progress is fears, the most common of which are fear of failure and fear of rejection. The fear of failure prevents you from making decisions to get out of your comfort zone. You provide yourself with feeble and convenient excuses to stay put. After all, if you don't do anything it's impossible for you to fail, so why do something and risk failure. When you are griped by fear of rejection, your anxiety is centered on the possibility of not being accepted or believed.

Staying in your comfort zone is so entrenched a habit that change to many people is virtually impossible if not already impossible. Your diehard habit ensures you are unwilling to change or give up your ideas or ways of behaving, even when there are good reasons to do so. You would rather remain in the same position and allow the continued existence of the negative and unhelpful circumstances you are in.

Once you are in the comfort zone, you lack the inspiration to do or want more. Even when you are not happy with your present circumstances, or you need or want something very much, you are unwilling to take risks in order to change them or get what you want. So what is happening here is that you are doing what you have always done and getting what you have always got.

It's up to you to act now and decisively to free yourself from the comfort zone. Once out of it, you begin to develop, expand and progress until without awareness, you lapse into another comfort zone and the cycle begins. It's up to you to stagnate, or grow and develop.

## 2. IF YOU START TAKING INVENTORY OF YOU, CAN YOU DEFINE YOURSELF? DO YOU KNOW WHERE YOU ARE GOING? ARE YOU CHALLENGING YOURSELF? WHAT DECISIONS YOU ARE WILLING TO MAKE TO CHANGE YOUR LIMITING BELIEFS. IT'S TIME TO GET OUT OF YOUR COMFORT ZONE. FIND WAYS AND THE RESOURCES YOU NEED TO IMPROVE YOURSELF. DECIDE TO BE YOUR BEST TODAY. YOU CAN, YOU WILL AND YOU MUST. SET NEW STANDARDS AND GO FOR WHAT YOU DESERVE.

Every year, you have the opportunity to audit yourself. But unfortunately, most people plunge into New Year's Eve focusing only on their shiny new goals.

"I'm going to start working out."

"I'm going to have better work-life balance."

"I'm going to get a handle on my finances."

The hard part is questioning how and why that goal didn't get achieved in the first place. Setting goals is easy. It's also fun to talk about. Pay attention to how many people share their goals and intentions for the New Year, but fail to explain how exactly they're going to get there.

But change doesn't happen easily, and it certainly doesn't happen overnight.

If you want to improve this year, you need to take the time to audit your current lifestyle and day-to-day habits.

Can you be successful in life? Of course! The unique combination of desire, planning, effort and perseverance will always work its magic. The question is not whether the formula for success will work, but rather whether you will work the formula. That is the unknown variable. That is the challenge that confronts us all.

We can all go from wherever we are to wherever we want to be. No dream is impossible provided we first have the courage to believe in it.

Here is how you can do that:

## Admit your mistakes.

Sometimes you have to admit them to others. Here's one of the best phrases in the English language: "I'm sorry." Those words could start a whole new relationship. They could start two people going in a whole new direction. Admit your mistakes to yourself. You don't have to babble about them to everyone in the neighborhood.

## Believe in yourself.

You've got to believe in the possibilities. You've got to believe that tomorrow can be better than today. Believe in yourself. There isn't a skill you can't learn; there isn't a discipline you can't try; there isn't a class you can't take; there isn't a book you couldn't read.

### Refine your goals.

Start the process. Set some higher goals. Reach for some higher purpose. Go for something beyond what you thought you could do.

### Ask for wisdom.

Ask for wisdom that creates answers. Ask for wisdom to deal with the challenges for today and tomorrow. Don't wish it was easier; wish you were better.

### Live with intensity.

You might as well turn it up a notch or two. Invest more of you in whatever you do. Be a little stronger; be a little wiser. Step up your vitality contribution. Put everything you've got into everything you do and then ask for more vitality, more strength and more vigor, more heart and more soul.

### Do something different

If you zig when others zag you will avoid being in the majority making it easier to rise to the top. It's far easiest to be great in a smaller pool.

### Who are you?

Character is who you are when nobody is looking. Be more concerned with your character than your reputation, because your character is what you really are while your reputation is merely what others think you are.

**Humility.**

Treat people how you want to be treated. Whether you acknowledge the cleaner tidying up your mess in the hotel or the CEO of your company, humility and sincere interest are ubiquitous in revealing you humanity.

# 3. TURN YOUR LIFE INTO A MASTERPIECE BY FOCUSING ON YOUR STRENGTHS. IF YOU'RE HERE TODAY AND NOT BEING SATISFIED, IT'S BECAUSE YOU HAVE NOT EXPLORED YOUR TALENTS YET. DEDICATE SOME TIME TO BE BETTER AND BE CONSISTENT BY DOING WHAT YOU'RE GOOD AT. BE INSPIRED, START MOVING TOWARDS YOUR DREAM LIFE. LET IT GO AND START FRESH. TODAY WILL BE A BETTER DAY.

Are you achieving the results you want from everything you do? If not, maybe it's time to ask yourself the following questions:

- Are you focusing on the right things?
- Is your energy and focus divided?
- Do you know what your strengths are?

Focusing on too many things at once will not enable you to achieve your best results. But even more important than that is to ensure that your focus is on what you do best, this is when you will do your best work and get your best results.

## Positive Psychology.

Martin Seligman, the father of Positive Psychology says that for a person to be truly happy and live a meaningful life, that person must recognize their personal strengths and use these strengths for the greater good. If we are to take Seligman's advice, we should spend time trying to figure out our personal strengths and not waste our valuable time and life doing jobs that don't please us and take us away from doing what we were made to do. If this is the secret of happiness, shouldn't we all be focusing on our strengths and not wasting time with all the other bits?

## Pareto Principle.

The Pareto Principle shows how filtering what you focus on can help towards more success. The Pareto Principle or the 80/20 rule is widely recognized as a principle which holds true in many facets of life. Sales executives use it to identify their important customers. They know that 20% of their customers give them 80% of their revenue and that 20% of their products will also give them 80% of the revenue. The clever know that once they identify that 20% they should focus their attention on that 20%. In this way results will be achieved more quickly and effectively.

If you focus most of your energy and attention on the important customers, this well reap rewards for your bank balance. Your good customers will become great customers. If you apply this principle to your whole life, if you were to focus solely on what you do best just imagine the results. If you were to stop doing the work that doesn't add value, the work that someone else could do for you. By directly focusing all your energy on your strengths, this will surely get you the results you aim for more quickly.

So if you don't know already, spend some time figuring out what your strengths are, what activity induces flow for you? When you know what activity it is, focus on it and do it to the best of your ability. Make sure you "only do what only you can do", focus on your 20%, and let others do the 80% of the work that you don't need to do. By doing this, not only will you be more efficient, creative, and productive, you will be happier and more successful.

## 4. WHAT IF YOU JUST BELIEVE YOU CAN MAKE MIRACLE HAPPEN IN YOUR LIFE WITHOUT WAITING PATIENTLY AROUND? WHAT IF YOU JUST THINK YOU CAN CHANGE YOUR STATE FROM DEPRESSION, ANXIETY, AND HOPELESSNESS TO JOY AND MAKE IT HAPPEN? CHANGE YOUR LIFE BY TAKING CONTROL OF YOUR THOUGHTS. STAY FOCUS ON YOUR ACCOMPLISHMENTS AND MORE WILL HAPPEN. BELIEVE IN YOURSELF. FIND GLORY WITHIN YOU. THE TIME IS NOW. DO NOT SETTLE FOR LESS ANYMORE. YOU'RE YOUR THOUGHTS.

To have control over your life, you have to accept that you are responsible for everything that happens to you. If you are a successful person, you know you are responsible and accept the full consequences of your action and behavior. If you are not, you are liable to believe fate causes and controls all events that happen to you, so that you cannot change or control the way things happen.

Acceptance of personal responsibility begins with feeling strongly that you are responsible for all areas of your life, especially emotionally and physically. If you can accept and firmly believe this, you are in a good position for real accomplishment of all your aims or purposes in life. If however you think whatever happen to you is beyond your control, you passively allow an external power to decide or fix what will happen to you in a way that you cannot change or control. You let your life follow blindly a preordained path.

Everything happens as a result of a particular action. If you can understand the reason why something happens to you, you can take control over its cause and effect. What cause everything that happens to you are principally your thoughts and beliefs. You are responsible for choosing what to think or believe. If you think positively of a desirable outcome, that desired outcome will be realized. If you believe in a negative outcome, you will produce the unsuccessful end result.

You owe it to yourself to be wholly responsible for thinking and believing positively or confidently about yourself. When you believe strongly in your ability to attain your objectives, you will be driven to accomplish them. Your high expectations are just as important. When you are highly and cautiously optimistic in your expectations, there's an excellent chance that they will be fulfilled. You build up your expectations, so do it in a responsible manner.

Your actions and attitudes result from your habits and beliefs that are firmly fixed in you. It's your responsibility to strengthen and practice your good habits, and discard entirely the old habits however difficult and replace them with good ones. Form a habit of associating yourself with only positive-thinking people and avoid completely those who constantly think negatively.

Take control of your life by controlling your thoughts and accepting responsibility for all the things that happen in your life. If you believe you are totally controlled by outside forces such as fate, you are always under their power and it's up to you to regain control of your life.

## 5. WE ARE ALL TRAINED TO FOCUS ON OUR IMPERFECTIONS. BY DOING SO, WE ARE NOT ABLE TO FOCUS ON OUR TALENTS. AS YOU GOING THROUGH YOUR DAY FIND OUT WHAT YOU'RE MADE OF AND GOOD AT. PICK ONE AREA OF YOUR LIFE TO GET BETTER AT IT. DO NOT GET DISTRACTED. TRAIN YOUR MIND TO SERVE YOU. DO NOT BE A SLAVE OF YOUR OWN MISERY. STOP TRYING TO FIT IN EVERYONE ELSE'S SHOES. LEARN ABOUT YOURSELF AND GROW. MIND YOUR LIFE ON A DAILY BASIS.

Self-mastery is about exercising complete control over your own self, especially your thoughts, emotions or behavior. Mastering yourself—your body and mind is a lifelong struggle. Besides maintaining control over what you think and believe, and how you feel, the pursuit of inner calm is an indispensable part of having mastery over self. When you aim to achieve absolute control of your own life, you have to have self-discipline, which is an essential element in self-mastery. Cultivate self-discipline first before you attempt at gaining self-mastery.

One of the important lessons to learn to gain self-mastery is to think positively. Once you start to think positively, you can then begin the process of achieving because you have to feel good before you can do anything good. The more positive you become, the more you tend to believe in your ability to attain great success. But merely thinking positively is not effective in itself. You have to take positive action. Every moment, guard against harmful thoughts entering your mind. This you do by refraining yourself from thinking such negative thoughts, which can seriously undermine your confidence in your attempts at attaining mastery of your mind.

Habitual wrong thoughts and strongly held mistaken beliefs have always been a source of feelings of negativity to many people. You owe it to yourself to banish every wrong thought and false belief that have for so long impeded your progress of getting better at doing or achieving something. Replace the wrong beliefs that you are not intelligent enough, rich enough, tall enough or fit enough to obtain the desired outcome. You can achieve as much as other people. You possess all the required qualities. But you are unaware of them or have not developed them to their true potential.

You know you are in complete control of your own life when you can consistently exercise unwaveringly strong personal discipline. This is reflected in your ability to proceed to do something completely that you have to do but do not feel like doing, as well as restrain yourself from doing something that you must not do but feel like doing. Discipline allows you to think in a right way, make the rightful choice and reject undesirable behavior. Use your discipline to think about the things you want, not those that you don't want.

Persist every day to develop yourself and your potential. Learn to manage your emotions when you are faced with adverse circumstances. It is a test of the degree of self-mastery you have acquired. When you are able to express a calm and confident feeling in dealing with a difficult situation while others panic, you can rest assured that you have reached a high level of self-mastery. You have really excelled yourself with each passing day.

If you want to improve other people, you must learn to improve yourself first. Likewise, if you want to change the world, you must first change yourself. It's always inside-out. Start off by controlling your thoughts. Cultivate the habit of thinking only of happy thoughts and you will feel happy on the outside. Mental conditioning is useful whenever you want to develop a quality. It's an effective way to achieve self-mastery.

## 6. IT'S TIME TO FOCUS ON YOU. THIS IS A NEW DAY WITH A NEW YOU. LET GO OF THE STRUGGLES OF THE PAST TO FACE YOUR DAY. JUST THINK YOU ARE ONE OF THE LUCKY ONES TO MAKE IT ALIVE TODAY. YOU OWE IT TO YOURSELF TO FEEL GOOD. TAKE ANOTHER APPROACH TO YOUR PAIN AND TURN YOUR LIFE AROUND.

We've all been there. You've just made a huge step forward in your life or achieved a vital goal, and want to tell everyone you know. You're bursting with pride and happiness and want to spread the joy. But have you ever stopped to listen to that little voice in your head that wonders whether or not the recipients of your great news really care? Sure, they might be listening to the words coming out of your mouth. They may even ask you questions. But at the end of the day, do they really care about you and your life?

### The harsh reality that will set you free.

Humans are a curious species in every sense of the world. They do strange things, and they are intrigued by the lives of others. This can lull you into a false sense of security and make you believe that they truly care for you and would be willing to help you out in times of need. In reality, most people do not really care for your well-being on a deep and meaningful level. When they take an interest in your engagement, for example, they may well be interested in the color scheme you'll choose for your wedding or where the proposal took place. However, most people are not going to be around to lend you emotional support when you start arguing with your spouse or feel overwhelmed by the prospect of spending every Christmas from now until eternity with your in-laws.

### Why you need to focus on making yourself happy.

Once you realize that most people keep their interactions on a fairly superficial level, you realize that self-reliance and the ability to make yourself happy is one of the most important skills you can develop. Aside from a few close friends and relatives, the majority of people you meet will simply not be around to lend you a listening ear when you get fired or are made redundant, even if they were excited when you landed that job in the first place.

You need to learn how to value your own talents and achievements because no one will ever care about your life nearly as much as you. When you are faced with a decision in life and are considering your next steps, listen to your intuition and act in accordance with your deepest desires. When you live a life truly on your own terms, you will be able to enjoy sharing good news secure in the knowledge that despite the fact no one much cares, you are achieving your own goals and fulfilling your unique vision of what a good life looks like.

## 7. A DISTRESSED MOMENT CAN COST YOU PAIN FOR A MOMENT OR FOR A LIFE TIME IF YOU ARE NOT ABLE TO PROCESS WELL THE INFORMATION AT HAND. YOUR MIND IS BY DEFAULT NOT THERE TO MAKE YOU HAPPY. IT REQUIRES TRAINING AND SPECIAL EFFORT TO CREATE AND BUILD THE LIFE YOU WANT. TO BE GOOD AT SOMETHING OR ANYTHING YOU HAVE TO PRACTICE AND BE CONSISTENT. THEREFORE, PRACTICE WHAT YOU ARE GOOD AT. DO NOT HOLD ON TO YOUR PAIN AND SUFFERING FOR TOO LONG. SEEK HELP IF YOU NEED. REVIEW YOUR OPTIONS.

Does your mind produce unhappy or happy thoughts?

Sometimes, we think it's our genes that make us the kind of person we are. However, that's not the whole story. Often we are so preoccupied with the status quo that we forget we have the power to become the person we want to be.

You have an estimated 70,000 thoughts per day. That's 70,000 chances to build yourself up or tear yourself down.

If you call yourself names, doubt your abilities, and second-guess your decisions, you'll harm your performance (and most likely you'll also be risking your physical and psychological health). But the good news is, you can change the way you think.

If happiness is what you're after, know that by training your mind you can program your mind to make you happy. And let's face it, who is not looking to be happy?

Here's how you can start instilling happy thoughts in your mind:

## Differentiate between ruminating and problem-solving.

Thinking about strategies that would help you overcome an obstacle is helpful, but imagining yourself unable to tolerate pain isn't productive. Whenever you find yourself thinking about something for an extended time, take a minute to think whether you're ruminating or problem-solving.

If you're actively solving or preventing problems, keep processing. But, if you're simply rehashing things that already happened or making catastrophic predictions about things you can't control, change the channel. Get up and do something to get your mind off the issue and keep your brain focused on more productive activities.

## Balance your emotions with logic.

Whether you're faced with a tough financial decision, or you're experiencing a family dilemma, you'll make your best decisions when you're able to balance your emotions with logic. When your emotions are running high, take steps to increase your rational thinking.

The best way to balance out your emotions is to create a list of the pros and cons of your choices. Reading over that list can help take some of the emotion out of the decision and equip you to make the best decisions.

## Subconscious re-training and inner healing.

Sometimes in order to become more positive, we have to uncover and then release the past negative experiences that we've been holding onto. Exercises like tapping, daily affirmations, neuro-linguistic programming, and mirror work can help you discover and heal these wounds. Additionally, these exercises can help you build a more supportive and affirming belief system that you can use the next time you face any traumatic experiences.

## Practice gratitude.

Gratitude has been linked to a host of physical and psychological benefits, including happiness. One study even found that grateful people are 25 percent happier.

So whether you make it a habit to talk about what you're grateful for over breakfast every morning, or you write in a gratitude journal before bed, train your brain to look for the good in life. It could be the simplest, yet most effective way to boost your well-being.

## Create a Healthy Mindset

The conversations you have with yourself have a profound effect on your life. If you want to reach your greatest potential, it's important to build your mental muscle. Exercise your brain every day and over time, you'll train your brain for happiness and success.

# 8. WAKE UP TODAY WITH SOME NEW DETERMINATION, TAKE CHARGE OF YOUR LIFE. LIVE LIKE YOU MEAN IT. ENOUGH OF SADNESS AND PAIN. TURN YOUR LIFE AROUND AND BE THE BEST VERSION OF YOURSELF NOW. YOU DESERVE BETTER. GO FOR IT. YOU ARE NOT DEAD. LIVE WITH PASSION.

Passion is the human equivalent of the fuel that powers your car. In a similar way passion powers a lifetime of dreams. It is an energy source for living an inspired life that is driven by purposeful action. In more specific terms passion is your vision for your life based on your core values, strengths, skills, interests and talents. With it, you can overcome any obstacle, solve any problem, and circumnavigate the endless challenges that life throws your way. Without it, people often succumb to anger, frustration, and disappointment and continuously get caught up in seemingly insurmountable problems.

### The Advantages of Living with Passion.

It is said that money often follows passion, and yet most people tend to chase money first and foremost and then wonder why they make very little progress. Whether there is truth to this argument or not, there are a number of other things that are worth considering when it comes to cultivating your passions.

Passion is, of course, a form of energy that tends to improve our focus and self-confidence as we work in the pursuit of our desired aims. Passionate people are focused because they have clarity about what they want to do, be, have and achieve in life. And because they have this clarity, this helps build self-confidence in their daily choices, decisions, and actions.

Tips on how to live life with passion and purpose:

## Make your life more meaningful.

Are you living a meaningful life? Is your life all about checking updates on social media? Is your life all about work and chasing to pay bills? Is your life bored and directionless?

People don't feel purposeful and they are not living with passion when they don't the life that they desire. Hence, you must create meanings to your life.

You have to define your ideal life, live it and make it meaningful.

## Don't compare yourself with others.

You should stop comparing yourself with others. How others live their life has nothing to do with you. Most people try to compare themselves with their colleagues and friends. They want to know who is doing much better. Who is earning more and who is driving a better car?

Don't, stop comparing yourself with others. You can be poor and at the bottom of your career right now. However, that does not mean that you will be at the bottom forever.

## Practice journaling.

There are plenty of benefits you can get from journaling. Not only that it can boost your creativity, journaling helps strengthen your self-discipline and able to evoke mindfulness.

## Meditate.

If you want to make your life purposeful, try meditation. And like journaling, meditation brings in a lot of great benefits to your life.

Albert Einstein once said that "Imagination is more important than knowledge", and he is absolutely right.

When you meditate, you are practicing how to actively directing your thoughts. You are cultivating the power of visualization.

## Enjoy the moment.

Live in the present. Your thoughts are not you. Stop worrying too much about your future or concern too much about your past. What matters most right now, is this present moment.

## Work on your goals.

One of the best ways to live a purposeful life is to work on your goals. Studies have shown that people feel the most satisfied and fulfilled when they are working toward a worthy ideal.

If you want to feel happy and satisfy, do something that will move you forward. This is especially true if the goal you are chasing is aligned with your purpose.

# 9. YES IT CAN BE PAINFUL. WHEN YOU NEED TO MAKE A DECISION TO TURN YOUR LIFE AROUND YOU HAVE TO KNOW HOW TO ENDURE PAIN BETTER. OTHERWISE THE CONSEQUENCES CAN LAST FOREVER. DO NOT BE FOOL BY A PAINFUL MOMENT. IT SHALL PAST. DEAL WITH IT AND TAKE CHARGE. YOU ARE STRONGER THAN YOUR PAIN. DO NOT LET YOUR MIND TRICK YOU THAT YOU ARE TOO WEAK TO DEAL WITH IT. DO NOT GET CONFUSE BETWEEN PAIN AND SUFFERING. SINCE THE FIRST ONE IS INEVITABLE AND THE LATTER IS A CHOICE. LEARN FROM YOUR PAIN AND GROW FROM IT. LIVE BETTER. THE TIME IS NOW.

There is no other area in our life where we choose pain as much as we do in the form of intense exercise. Think about it, for those of us that have the real love for exercise, we seem to have some sort of masochistic connection to it. "It hurts so good" we say!  "No pain, no gain" we shout!

We actually pay money for classes and trainers that practically torture us and we love it. It's true, to build muscle we must first break muscle. It is a physiological fact. A design from God Himself.

What we get from this truth is a strong life lesson that we must apply to all areas of our true health.

In order to "grow" in our mindset and in our spiritual life we must endure some pain and accept change. We must dig deep and get uncomfortable and persevere through some pretty tough times in order to get the ultimate reward of greater health and a greater life.

How can we do this intentionally? It is slightly different than the pain you get from exercise, because often the emotional pain we may seek won't have that wonderful "endorphin" high that exercise has nor will be it be over in the 45-min time frame that every good solid workout should fit.

A goal for your mindset might be something like reading a certain number of books in a month or year about thing you are struggling with or just want to learn more. It might also be to take the risk a seek that guidance counselor or therapist to deal with that thing from your past your been subconsciously avoiding and "numbing" yourself from your whole life.

## 10. IF YOU KNOW TODAY WOULD BE THE LAST DAY OF YOUR LIFE WHAT WILL YOU DO DIFFERENTLY? SOME PEOPLE GO THROUGH LIFE LIKE THEY WILL BE HERE FOREVER, THEY HAVE NO IDEA ABOUT THEIR NEXT MOVE. THEY LIVE LIKE THEIR EXISTENCE HAVE NO VALUE ON EARTH. IF YOU ARE ONE OF THOSE PEOPLE, I'M TELLING YOU IT'S TIME TO START LIVING, NOBODY KNOWS WHEN WILL BE THEIR LAST DAY. TODAY IS YOUR DAY TO MAKE A SIMPLE CONTRIBUTION TO THE WORLD. YOU ARE A GIFT TO THE WORLD. YOU'RE UNIQUE, YOU HAVE TALENTS. BE ON THE QUEST TO DISCOVER THEM AND PUT THEM TO WORK. MAKE A DIFFERENCE IN THE LIFE OF SOMEONE. FEEL FREE TO SHARE A SMALL GESTURE THAT YOU ARE COMMITTED TO DO.

To make the most out of your life, you need to keep on improving its quality. Once you live your life to the fullest, you start being happier which means you have a higher chance of achieving your goals.

## Overcome Your Fear.

We all have fears and phobias even if we don't speak much about them. However, just a few of us work on overcoming them. Instead, we try not to do things that scare us. Although it seems obvious to avoid doing things that are connected to our phobias, it's important to remember that fears limit your success as you don't do the things you might like. No matter what fear you have, try to overcome it in order to prove yourself that it's you who is in charge of your destiny. Stop living in a fear of something; it's time to enjoy your life.

## Establish Strong Relationships.

Communication plays an important role in the social life, and everyone has a big number of people he is communicating with. The level of your communication affects your well-being, and it's significant to build good relations with people.

## Stop Blaming Yourself for Mistakes.

Nobody loves making mistakes, but it's in our nature to do amiss. Most people blame themselves for mistakes, and it negatively affects their mental health. If you want to keep on living a happy life, you need to learn from your failures but don't be obsessed with them.

The main idea is that you cause depression and stress when you're blaming yourself, and it prevents from living a better life. Once you accept failures and work on improving your life, you become a happier person.

## Prioritize experiences over objects.

Time and time again, you'll find that people towards the ends of their lives regret only a few simple things: not spending more time with their families and not experiencing more of life. They regret spending so much time in the office or trying to accumulate things versus actually putting what they've earned towards experiences.

A key to your best life? Actually living it. Go on trips. See the world. Go to concerts and films. Road trip with your family. Do things you've always wanted to do and see things you've always wanted to see. They're things you'll never regret! Making memories is always, always better than buying an object.

## Live intentionally.

Lastly, the best way to live a good life is to live it intentionally. Whether it's in what you eat or how you exercise or in the way you deal with the people around you, be intentional. In short, strive to be the person that you truly hope to be in all things. That growth only happens when we're intentional about it.

If you have a fitness goal, you have to make a conscious effort to go to the gym and to eat well. If you want to forge a better relationship in your life, it means spending time with that person.

But more than just personal goals, living intentionally means soaking in life. It means appreciating the things around you, whether big or small. It means seeing small glories in the sunset and the stars and appreciating a spring breeze and birdsong. It means being able to stop and take joy in what's around you.

Living your best life, if anything, is about that: never taking anything for granted.

## CHAPTER 7

# YOU ARE BLESSED

I T'S NEVER TOO LATE. Don't focus on what was taken away. Find something to replace it, and acknowledge the blessing you have.

## 1. MOST OF YOUR DISAPPOINTMENTS ARE BASED ON YOUR EXPECTATIONS ON OTHER PEOPLE. DO NOT SET YOURSELF FOR FAILURE AND BECOME ANGRY AT OTHERS. MAKE AN EFFORT TO BE MORE THAN AVERAGE. BE YOUR BEST TODAY AND SHARE YOUR EXPERIENCE WITH PEOPLE THAT CAN UNDERSTAND YOU. DO NOT LOWER YOUR STANDARDS TO

# MEET OTHER PEOPLE'S NEEDS EVEN WHEN YOU LIVE UN-HAPPY. MAKE BETTER CHOICES. KNOW WHAT YOU DE-SERVE. LOVE YOURSELF ABOVE ALL. YOU ARE BEAUTIFUL!

Every day, whether you like it or not, you have to make choices for your future self. Whether it's about where you'll be living next year or how you'll spend your money, making tough decisions is something that is bound to happen. Before you make a big decision, though, there are a few things you should consider.

There's no doubt that making choices on your own can be a very scary thing. What happens if you make the wrong one? This is the question that goes through your head every time you are faced with a huge choice to make. But it's best not to live in fear, so here are some ways for you to make better decisions without the help of others. While it's tempting to ask for advice for every big decision you have to make in your life, you need to practice making decisions by yourself and trust your own thoughts and actions. Once you start loving the decisions you're making, you won't need the approval of others.

## Be aware of what you want.

The best way to make a decision is by knowing what your goals are. When you're more aware of what you want out of your life, you may be able to make better choices. People who aren't self-reflective are going to end up making bad decisions because they don't really know what they want in the first place. When you try to make a decision, always think about where you want to be in a year. Will this affect your life in a negative way? Is this the direction you want to go? If the answer is against what you are working towards, then try to change your decision, even if that means taking the harder route.

### Listen to your gut.

Whether you believe it or not, you probably already know yourself better than you realize. But sometimes, you ignore what your gut is telling you because you may not want to face the reality of the decision you have to make.

### Make sure you are in the right frame of mind.

It's easy to make poor decisions when you're in a bad mood, especially when you're hungry, sleepy, or stressed. But when it comes to life-changing decisions, try to make sure you're feeling comfortable and at ease before you decide what your next move is going be.

### Learn to trust yourself.

Don't be afraid to trust yourself. The person you need to trust first is yourself. No one can be as consistently supportive of you as you can learn to be. Being kind to yourself increases self-confidence and lessens your need for approval. Loving and caring for yourself not only increases self-trust, it also deepens your connection with others. Having the confidence to trust yourself is a task on its own, but once you have more confidence in yourself, you may feel better about making big decisions in the future.

## 2. THE MOMENT YOU BELIEVE IN YOUR POTENTIAL YOU

# START FINDING OPPORTUNITIES TO MAKE YOUR DREAMS COME TRUE. IT IS IMPORTANT TO MAKE AN EFFORT TO CONNECT WITH YOURSELF AND DISCOVER YOUR TALENTS. YOU CAN ACCOMPLISH MUCH MORE THAN YOU THINK. START HAVING A PLAN FOR YOUR LIFE TO BECOME AMAZING. IT'S NOT TOO LATE. YOUR REGRET WON'T TAKE YOU TOO FAR, START MAKING A MEMORY FOR YOUR TOMORROW.

Potential is something that is inherent in you that makes you achieve your purpose. It is a raw material that can be transformed into money spinning benefit.

## The Orange Seed Analogy.

The orange is characterized by not just a seed, but multiple seeds. Basically, if all things being equal, the seeds are potential trees. For instance, if an orange contains 15 seeds, it holds that we have 15 potential trees and these 15 trees will produce fruits with seeds. The trend goes on and on. It simply means that one orange has great potentials of generations of seeds and trees. In the same vein, you are endowed with lots of potentials that can make you live an exceptional life because it works by the multiplier effect.

Your potential is closely related with your passion and purpose. Your potential is what you do effortlessly without stress. It is the thing you do passionately and joyfully without being paid.

However, potential is just like raw materials that needs to be worked upon, refined and polished. Gold can't be gold if didn't pass through fire. Crude oil will never roll in billions of dollars if it remained as crude and didn't undergo further processing.

## Steps To Discover Your Life Potentials

### Understand Your Heart Connection.

You look, and will always look like your mind. Therefore, if you must discover your potential, first answer the question of the mind, "what is the deepest desire of your heart?"

Most times, your heart's desire is your life desire. Your life desire is the key to what you really want in destiny.

Many dreams are shattered, not because they are hired or cheaper, just because they are not ordered. Understand your heart connection. That's where it all begins.

### Understand your passion.

Action needs passion, or it will be sanctioned. Understand your passion and let it find expression. The second step to discover your potential is to find out what stirs your passion. What stirs your passion?

### Understand what gives you joy.

This is the third step to discover your potential. It is a very simple truth you must not fail to tell yourself. What do you enjoy doing most that give you energy? Remember, telling yourself the truth is honesty and telling others is integrity.

The truth you tell yourself here is what will determine your level of self-discovery and fulfillment.

### Understand your natural ability.

Having understood your passion and what gives you joy, it is time to understand what you are naturally able to do. The truth of the matter is that, whatever you were designed and manufactured to do will feel natural when you do it.

Can you quickly answer this question, what naturally flows out of you?

### Understand what you do well.

Ever wondered how you achieve what take others time easily? That's exactly what I am talking about. Although others find it complex, it will be simple for you. Jot down the gifts that people commend you for. Know where you produce good results without stress.

Ask yourself. "What do people say I do well?"

### Understand your dreams.

Your dream is what determines your drive. The best time to dream is when your eyes are open in the early morning. Begin to find out the ideas, visions, and dreams that are impossible to get out of your mind.

# 3. WE HURRY SOMETIMES TO GO TO THE TOP AND ONCE WE GET THERE WE REALIZE WE HAD NO PLAN TO STAY ON TOP. TAKE YOUR TIME TO PLAN AND MEASURE YOUR OUTCOMES. DO WHAT'S RIGHT, THE RIGHT WAY, AT THE RIGHT TIME WITHOUT PRESSURE. YOU ARE VALUABLE NO MATTER

# HOW DIFFICULT IS YOUR CURRENT SITUATION. YOU ARE DESIGNED TO GROW IN LIFE. KEEP LEARNING AND LEARN TO BE FLEXIBLE. FIND WAYS TO INCREASE VALUE TO YOUR LIFE. GO BEYOND YOUR LIMITED THINKING. DO WHAT OTHERS THINK IT'S IMPOSSIBLE. PROVE THEM WRONG BY REACHING TO YOUR TRUE POTENTIAL.

Becoming a more flexible person reflects the same things. Flexibility can help you deal with all kinds of life situations. It can even lead to adventure and learning.

Being able to "go with the flow" and be flexible in your thinking is a necessary skill for dealing with life's inevitable changes. This is a trait that helps us adjust more easily to new circumstances, challenges and situations as they arise. Whether it's starting a new job, taking a new class or getting married, being cognitively flexible helps us to grow and get along better with others.

However, for many people, this is much easier said than done — especially for those who tend to "get stuck" on certain thoughts and behaviors patterns. They may also tend to be stubborn, argumentative or oppositional, worry constantly, get upset when things don't go their way, be uncooperative (or automatically say "no" to things), or have conditions such as addictions, obsessive compulsive tendencies, eating disorders and even road rage. A common feature of all of these is difficulty letting go of thoughts or behaviors.

If you are wondering how to become more flexible in life, here are some of the most effective tips you can try.

### Stretch your brain.

When you engage your imagination and problem-solving skills, it's like training and preparing your brain to adapt to **slow or sudden life situations.**

### Thought Stopping.

An important part of gaining control over your repetitive thoughts is to become aware of them when they occur—and then practice the simple technique of thought stopping. The more you practice this, the more you get control over your thoughts. You can also use a rubber band on your wrist and snap it when you catch yourself in a loop of negative thinking.

### Write Out Options and Solutions.

Writing down your thoughts helps to "get them out of your head" and allows you to view them more rationally. You can do this:

Write down the thought that is stuck in your head

Write down what you can do to help offset the thought

Write down the things that you have no control over with regard to the thought

### Think Before Automatically Saying "No".

Some people have the tendency to say "no" automatically—even before thinking about what was asked of them. This can be especially problematic in relationships. It is limiting and unnecessary to always dismiss ideas or deny your partner his or her requests. To help with this, take a deep breath, hold it for three seconds, and then take five seconds to exhale, while actually considering what the best way to respond would be.

Using these techniques can help you improve your mental flexibility which in turn can help reduce your worries, improve your relationships and reduce the distress you experience when you get stuck on unhealthy or negative thoughts and behaviors.

## 4. IF YOU DO NOT KNOW YOUR DESTINATION YOU WILL END SOMEWHERE THAT YOU DO NOT LIKE. STEP BY STEP YOU WILL ACHIEVE ANYTHING YOU WANT. MOST PEOPLE WANT MASSIVE RESULTS BY MAKING SIMPLE STEPS TOO QUICKLY AND GET DISCOURAGED. CONSISTENCY WILL LEAD TO GREATNESS. BE PERSISTENT AND BELIEVE THAT EVERY STEP YOU MAKE WILL LEAD YOU CLOSER TO YOUR DESTINATION. YOU MIGHT FEEL THAT YOU'RE NOT MOVING BUT KEEP ON GOING. DO NOT STOP. KEEP GOING. FOLLOW YOUR PATH OF SUCCESS THAT YOU DESIGNED. LEAVE YOUR INSECURITY BEHIND.

Persistence is probably one of the most admirable characters a person can possess. It's the ability to be determined to do or achieve something regardless of any setbacks. A distinguishing attributes of those who succeed in life against those who don't is persistence.

Many has the capacity to set goals and plans toward success, yet only few succeeds, because only few stick to work on their goals and plans until it is accomplished.

Majority stops before they even start or they quit in the middle of their journey. Oftentimes, the reason for quitting is hardships, discomfort and uncertainty. They let their fears and doubts paralyze them from moving persistently toward their goals. Or perhaps, their motivation isn't firm enough to drive them to work on it.

Developing persistence is a master skill to success. It is easier to relax and do nothing, or just live in our comfort zone, rather than face the uncertainty and discomfort of sailing through our goals. Plus, the idea of failure and hardship is unbearable. But if you want to create change in your life and achieve success, now is the time to develop and master persistence.

Here are the ways to help you develop persistence:

### Identify Your Wants and Desires.

Before you can develop persistence and eventually achieve success, you need to first identify your wants or desires. You can do this by simply writing down specifically all the things you want to have or accomplish. List down all your desires and wants, no matter how impossible they are to achieve in the moment.

### Outline Your Definite Action Step.

Identifying your wants or desires speaks of what you want to achieve. Determining your motivation shows the reasons why you want to achieve what you want. Outlining your definite action step is necessary to know how you will be able to achieve what you want.

When you know how to get what you want, it makes it easier to achieve it. To know how, it pays to do some research and planning of what needs to be done on your part. Be specific on each step you need to take. Identify at least two ways and plans on how you can achieve your goals.

### Keep a Positive Mental Attitude.

The road to success is not easy, in fact, it's challenging, this is why only few succeeds. There will be countless times you will be face with defeat and failures that if you are weak, you'll be succumbing to negative thoughts of fears and doubts.

In order to develop persistence and eventually succeed in your endeavor, always maintain a positive mental attitude, regardless of situation. Keep your thoughts focused on taking action towards your goals. Avoid negative thoughts and feelings for it will ruin your concentration and persistence.

### Develop Discipline and Habit.

All your goal-setting and planning will go to waste if you won't be able to develop discipline and good habit.

There will be a lot of hindrances that will stop you from moving towards your goal, and without proper discipline, it will be easy for you to sail away. Upholding discipline and good habits can help you stay in the course, even despite difficulties.

### Be Confident.

You should be confident in your work that you will achieve what you want. It's a long journey to fight for, many people will put you down, and obstacles are never ending. No matter how hard is the situation, believe in yourself, you are going to make it. Don't listen to what others said, most people don't think from your shoes.

## 5. IF YOU THINK YOUR WISHFUL THINKING AND IMAGINATION WILL LEAD YOU TO GREATNESS YOU ARE WRONG. YOUR ATTITUDE TOWARDS OBSTACLES AND YOUR ACTIONS WILL SURELY DRIVE SUCCESS IN YOUR LIFE. YOUR CHALLENGES ARE THERE TO STRETCH YOU TO DISCOVER YOUR POTENTIAL AND GO BEYOND THE NORM TO ACHIEVE VICTORY. CHOOSE TO BE COMFORTABLE IS CHOOSING TO BE MISERABLE AND LIVE A LIFE OF REGRET. IT'S NOT TOO LATE TO START. START ACTING NOW. EVERY SIMPLE STEP WILL LEAD YOU TO YOUR DESTINATION. YOU WILL BE GLAD YOU DID BY THE END OF THIS YEAR.

We are all faced with challenges constantly in every area of our lives. Most people have a hard time accepting and dealing with these challenges that arise. The truth is that you will have to deal with difficult problems throughout your life, whether it is in your personal life or career. Most of us get really afraid and run away from problems because we don't want to accept reality the way it is. Running away from your problems is the worst thing you can do to deal with the challenges you are faced with.

Here are some suggestions on ways to handle life's challenges in life:

## Move Toward The Challenge.

If your strategy is to avoid life's challenges, remember that the continual need for delusion will be huge. It will also suck up a great deal of your energy. It may seem easier at first to turn away, or pretend the problem is smaller than it really is. But, reality will rear its ugly head at some point in the future and you'll be forced to deal with the problem.

The closer we get to our challenge, the more we can educate ourselves about it. If we can get close enough to analyze it, we can assess which of our strengths will be needed to overcome it. The steps to follow and actions to take may not reveal themselves to us until we have moved closer to the situation. Mountain climbers understand that it's impossible to know where to place fingers and feet by looking at a mountain from the bottom. They find safety only when they get close enough to explore the cracks and crevices.

## Prepare To Take Action.

Life gives you a bad hand. What are you going to do? Move toward the challenge, cry like a baby, run away, or do nothing?

Our reaction is a test of character and it says a lot about us. Always remember that it doesn't matter what you've been given, what matters is what you do with it. Since we have layers of fear, often our first response is to exaggerate the situation and interpret life's challenges as a crisis. We become cautious, retreat, and hope for things to get better— all on their own. Parents who over-protect their kids from adversity reinforce that way of thinking. They swoop in and come to the rescue. As a result, their kids never have to analyze how to work it out for themselves. They do not have the opportunity to develop their strengths to compensate for their weaknesses.

## Move Past Self-Limiting Beliefs.

Most barriers are internal, not external. We make certain assumptions about ourselves and how life's challenges should be approached and solved. These thoughts produce self-limiting because they can trap us into an outmoded way of thinking about ourselves and our abilities.

The U.S. Army is using research that has shown most people, when confronted with adversity and the need to remove obstacles, will experience initial feelings of fear, frustration, and paralysis. Given sufficient amounts of time, however, they recover and continue to perform at the same level they were performing before the adversity.

# 6. LEARN TO IGNORE THE SMALL VOICES IN YOUR HEAD THAT KEEP YOU COMFORTABLE AND UNHAPPY. BELIEVE IN YOUR POTENTIAL. YOUR BEST DAY ARE BEHIND YOU, YOUR OPPORTUNITIES TO SHINE ARE ALSO THERE. LIFE IS FULL OF RICH POSSIBILITIES. DON'T JUST GROW BUT BLOOM. YOU NEED TO KEEP GOING NO MATTER WHAT OTHERS THINK OF YOU. MAKE SURE YOU'RE FACING THE RIGHT DIRECTION. MAKE YOUR TIME ON EARTH UNFORGETTABLE. DON'T JUST PASS BY, MAKE YOURSELF KNOWN.

Creating limits can cause barriers that will influence your levels of success in your personal life and at work. Assume your life is on a freeway, you cannot stay in one spot, and you must keep moving forward.

This might go against all you have ever known while growing up but the truth is, human lives are not governed by any defined limits. This means you can become an over achiever and at this height of success, there will still be numerous avenues for growth yet to be explored.

# WAYS TO REACH YOUR FULL POTENTIAL:

### Realize that hard work beats talent, when talent doesn't work hard.

Regardless of your situation, circumstances, ability or environment hard work will bring you results. If you are always prepared to be the hardest worker in any given room, good things are going to happen to you. It may take time, and it sure as hell won't be easy, but if you're prepared to get your hands dirty you will likely earn it.

### Realize that complacency is the enemy.

Complacency emerges when you create a comfort zone for yourself and remain in its walls. Some people may argue that it's good to be happy with what you have and that is true to a certain extent. However, the moment you become comfortable with where you are in life, you are never going to get to where you need to be.

Celebrate your success and don't be afraid to pat yourself on the back now and again, but realize that just as you're resting on your laurels, your competition will be nipping at your heals. People are always getting better and the moment you take your foot off the pedal you're opening up a path to be overtaken.

**Understand the truth behind the saying "Failure is the prerequisite to success".**

Have you ever failed at something big such as starting your own business, or something less significant like winning a competition? When you failed did you tell yourself you weren't good enough and gave up on the idea of ever trying again?

Take Thomas Edison for example, he failed at creating the light bulb over 10,000 times before he succeeded. Ten thousand times!

Please learn that failure is the path to success. Even more, being persistent and determined are non-negotiable, if you ever want to get close to achieving your potential.

**Develop an unstoppable internal drive.**

If you want to achieve and surpass what you believe to be your potential you must develop an insane unstoppable internal drive. You have to want to achieve your goals more than anything else in the world and be prepared to do whatever it takes on your quest to self-improvement. That is the only bulletproof way to reach your full potential.

# 7. BEFORE YOU START TO COMPLAIN ABOUT YOUR LIFE TODAY, THINK HOW BLESS YOU ARE TO HAVE A VOICE, NOT BEING IN THE HOSPITAL HOPING TO SURVIVE, ABLE TO WALK, SEE, TALK AND FEEL. LET'S START TO APPRECIATE THE GIFT OF "TODAY". EVERYTHING DOES NOT HAVE TO BE PERFECT TO START BEING HAPPY. PRACTICE DAILY TO REMOVE THE BARRIERS OF YOUR HAPPINESS AND LIVE LIFE

## TO THE FULLEST. STOP TAKING YOUR LIFE FOR GRANTED. YOU ARE BLESSED.

Amidst the hustle and bustle of modern life, do we ever stop to remember how good we have it? Do we ever stop to think about how lucky we are to live relatively normal lives in places that, at the surface at least, seem stable enough to support our work to create a new paradigm?

We're all in a great position to create the inner and outer changes that need to be made, and we could go about our work with a sense of gratitude for our existence if we could see that, in a sense, everything is exactly the way it's meant to be.

We have life, and every day we're given on this Earth is a blessing that we should not only appreciate, but utilize to the fullest extent.

Only when we can learn to love life can we share our love with the rest of the world, and until we repair everything in our life that keeps us from enjoying or appreciating it, we'll have trouble creating change in the world.

There are a lot of bad things to be said about this planet, but there are a lot of good things too. There are things here that most people don't even realize are around, because they never get out and expand their horizons.

Similarly, there are things we can find within that most people have failed to grasp or understand, much less explore with any kind of enthusiasm, and by accepting the opportunity we've been given, we can join the ranks of people throughout history who've pioneered the exploration of a greater reality.

When we can appreciate this existence, which is a blessing whether we realize it or not, we can open the inner doorway to higher vibrations, mystical wonders and an enhanced understanding of the oneness of all of creation.

We'll understand that we've been taking life way too seriously, and all the pressure we've put on ourselves is completely unnecessary.

Yes, survival is a serious matter and we're right to be concerned with sustaining ourselves, but beyond all of that, we're spiritual beings who've been put here to enjoy this world as we climb the spiral back into a higher existence.

The last thing we should be doing is running around like chickens with our heads cut off to support the very system that's keeping us enslaved.

We aren't here to try so hard, and we aren't here to be so stressed out. We're here to live. We're here to love, laugh, find joy in the simple things, help people when they need it the most, and use our gifts to make some kind of positive impact in the world, however small or humble.

We're here to enjoy everything life throws our way, and the great secret to life is that it doesn't have to be so mean, intimidating or unnecessarily difficult. It doesn't have to be a constant struggle to survive, and we don't have to bounce around from dramatic moment to dramatic moment.

When we find peace in our soul and we appreciate our existence, our entire outlook changes and we stop trying so hard to find the things that, as we're learning, require us to open our minds and ease up on the tension to find. We won't find anything within if we're tense or we try too hard, and this includes happiness.

When we are connected, we'll learn that self-care is as important as helping others and we aren't excluded from the people who deserve help. We can help ourselves while we help others, and giving ourselves the freedom to have fun will help us appreciate life even more.

Our appreciation will really increase once this connection is strong, and somewhere along the way, we'll teach others to appreciate life too. Eventually, the world will be full of world changers who appreciate their existence and are willing to work together to create a fairer, more sustainable way of life.

## 8. NO ONE BUT YOU ARE RESPONSIBLE OF THE RESULTS YOU WANT IN YOUR LIFE. NO RESULTS AND SATISFACTION WILL COME WITHOUT EFFORT, COMMITMENT AND CONSISTENCY. WE OFTEN FAIL TO REALIZE HOW CLOSE WE ARE TO SUCCEED AND GIVE UP TOO SOON. IF YOU HOLD ON TO FEAR FOR A MINUTE LONGER YOU CAN TURN IT INTO COURAGE. BE WILLING TO GO ONE STEP FURTHER TO GET WHAT YOU WANT. SOMETIME, THAT ALL IT TAKES TO WIN IT. TO HAVE WHAT YOU WANT IN LIFE HAVE THE WILL TO TRY IT ONCE MORE AND HAVE FAITH TO BELIEVE IT'S POSSIBLE.

*"Courage is not the absence of fear, but rather the judgment*

*that something else is more important than fear."*

**— MEG CABOT**

Rosa Parks. Mahatma Gandhi. Dr. Martin Luther King, Jr. Jackie Robinson. Alice Paul. The unknown rebel standing in front of Chinese tanks in Tiananmen Square.

Each one of these individuals stepped out of their comfort zone to stand up for what they believed was the right thing to do regardless of a lack of popular support or having a clear position of power. Each of these incidents dealt with civil liberties and a desire for justice that demanded the mustering up of courage and the willingness to place themselves in a situation where the outcome would be unknown. Due to the stance that each of these courageous people took they helped make the world a bit more accepting, a bit more just, and a bit more humane.

While these were grand and impressive acts of courage, let us not dismiss how we too can live courageously to improve our lives. After all, one must practice being courageous and be willing to step up to the plate whenever a moment presents itself, and being able to step up to the plate only gets easier with practice on smaller matters first. If we want a life of our dreams, rather than a life that is presented to us that we decide to settle for, we must live courageously.

### Gain knowledge.

Knowing something and having a credible source (or more—which is preferred) will build your confidence about what you know to be true.

### Stop procrastinating and give it a try.

Do your best. Learn from the results of that first attempt and do not become discouraged.

### Face what you fear.

Look it in the eye and determine what exactly it is that you are afraid of. Rejection? Being laughed at? Not being accepted? Often our fears are telling us what we desire the most in our lives, and it is up to us to listen to this internal message and follow that yearning.

### Take a step outside of your comfort zone.

By being open to meeting new people, visiting a new city that you don't know but are curious about, changing up your routine a bit or having a taste of something that you assumed wouldn't be to your liking, you are gradually strengthening your ability to be courageous.

### Practice Standing up for What you Believe is Right/Just/etc.

If your desire is to be able to have enough strength to stand up to those who are bullying you, don't allow others to be bullied either. In other words, practice standing up for others who need a helping hand. It is often easier to be courageous when someone else is in need, rather than standing up for ourselves. So by being clear about what you will and won't tolerate, learn how to find the gumption within yourself to have a voice when it is necessary. This will help you find your voice when you need to stand up for yourself.

### Be Disciplined.

In order to have self-discipline, you must be very clear about what you want, and thus, very clear about what you don't want. As you begin making progress toward what you do desire, you will be less easily swayed to go off course which will make it easier to display self-discipline, allowing you to proceed forward even if no one understands your efforts.

## Trust Yourself.

With each year of life experience, as you pour over what you enjoy versus what makes you cringe, what makes your heart sing versus what tears at your heartstrings, you hone your instincts. You begin to realize what is worth taking a risk for—love, a particular career, justice, etc. And when you know what is important to you, you begin to realize that you must choose what you care most about over the fear that stands in the way.

# 9. OUR OWN LIMITATIONS KEEP UP FROM RISING ABOVE OUR FEARS. WE OUGHT IT TO OURSELVES TO GO BEYOND OUR FEARS AND TAKE CHANCE TO GREATNESS. YOU HAVE TO BE WILLING TO SAIL WITH THE WIND AND SOMETIMES AGAINST IT TO FIND THE OPPORTUNITIES. TAKE MASSIVE ACTIONS AND YOU WILL HAVE LASTING SATISFYING RESULTS. GO FOR WHAT YOU WANT AND EMBRACE YOUR FEARS TO MOVE TO VICTORY.

During the pursuit of greatness negative or fearful thoughts always seem to come across our mind at one point or another. Whether it's those seemingly omnipresent thoughts that remind us of all the failures we've had in the past. Majority of us go through times where even the most confident of us has encountered some sort of self-doubt. Overcoming this doubt can be more challenging to some depending on the level of doubt we have.

In many cases what keeps many of us from reaching success is the reluctance to change and unwillingness to sacrifice. No matter the goal we have set for ourselves nine times out of ten we're going to have to sacrifice something to accomplish it. Whether it's time, money, sleep, hanging out with friends or lessening the time we spend on social media.

Many times in the effort to minimize stress we choose to take the "safe route" or don't take any risk whatsoever. Unfortunately, every human being on this earth no matter what race, color or background only lives once. Therefore, if we don't take any chances to live the life we truly want we can never get it back. A wise woman once said "You can always get different jobs, change careers, but you can never get time back... no matter how much money you have time is something none us can get back so you might as well spend your time doing something you actually love to do."

One of the easiest ways to overcome fear and self-doubt is to just do it. Sounds simple and easier said than done right? However, a method that has been used over the years is the 5 Second Rule. This rule can be utilized in any situation where fear or self-doubt plays a role. To apply the rule all you have to do is when fear or self-doubt starts to creep in stop everything you're doing count to 5 and clear your mind. After you count to five say five reasons why you can achieve your goal, five accomplishments you've made in the past and five positive qualities you like about yourself. This not only helps with your fear, but trains your mind to rid itself of those negative and limiting beliefs.

On our path to greatness we will most likely encounter some sort of negative thoughts, self-doubt or negative people. However, we have to keep our positive mindset, because in the end if we choose to give up on our dreams we will only regret it later.

## 10. WAKE UP AND OPERATE FROM A STATE OF MIND THAT WILL GIVE YOU ONLY POSITIVE RESULTS. STAY AWAY FROM NEGATIVITY AND PEOPLE WHO ARE DOWNERS. BE INFLUENCED BY PEOPLE IN YOUR FIELD AND FIND YOUR MOTIVATION TO GET YOU TO THE NEXT LEVEL. BE COMMITTED TO EXCELLENCE REGARDLESS OF YOUR CHOSEN FIELD. DON'T BE LAZY, SEATING AROUND EXPECTING GOOD RESULTS. MAKE IT HAPPEN NO MATTER WHAT. KNOW WHAT YOU DESERVE AND GO FOR IT. YOU ARE TALENTED; YOU ARE NOT SHINNING YET BECAUSE MORE POLISHING IS NEEDED. STICK TO WHAT YOU SAY AND GET IT DONE. BE A LEADER.

It's been said that one bad apple can spoil the whole bunch and often, that applies to the business environment. It's usually easy to identify that Negative Nancy or Debbie Downer who wreak havoc on morale. Their bad attitudes, catastrophic thinking, and fatalistic outlooks can infiltrate the ranks and spread like an epidemic.

Negative people can also cause problems for us on an individual level. Perhaps it's that vendor who causes you to grit your teeth. Or maybe it's a colleague whom you avoid at all costs. It's important to recognize when these negative individuals intrude in your life in an unwelcome manner.

Sometimes, we unknowingly give toxic individuals influence over our thoughts, behaviors, and feelings. Whether you spend two hours complaining about that boss you don't like, or you let an angry customer ruin your day, it's important to regain your personal power.

Here are some strategies to take back you power and reduce the detrimental impact negative people have in your life:

Negative people can monopolize your time—even when they're not with you—if you're not careful. It's easy to spend two hours dreading a one hour meeting with a negative person. Combine that with two hours of venting to a co-worker after the meeting, and you've just given that person five precious hours of your time.

Don't allow negative people to steal your time and energy. Rather than complain about people you don't enjoy, choose to strike up conversations about pleasurable topics. Similarly, instead of spending your commute thinking about how much you dislike that person you have to work with, turn on the radio and listen to music that reduces your stress. Take back your power by limiting the amount of time you spend talking about, thinking about, and worrying about unpleasant people.

## Choose Your Attitude

Spending time with negative people can be the fastest way to ruin a good mood. Their pessimistic outlooks and gloomy attitude can decrease our motivation and change the way we feel. But allowing a negative person to dictate your emotions gives them too much power in your life.

## Choose to Behave Productively.

Negative people can bring out the worst in us if we're not careful. Sometimes certain pessimists seem to have the power to raise our blood pressure, for one reason or another. A normally calm, mild-mannered person may resort to yelling when he can't take one more second of negativity. Or, after being surrounded by negative co-workers for hours, an optimist may find herself convincing others that the company's future is doomed.

## Seek Out Positive People.

It's difficult to look on the bright side when you're surrounded by negativity. Seek out positive people to keep you balanced. Just like negative people can rub off on you, a positive person can brighten your spirit.

Identify the positive people in your life. Proactively schedule time with them on a regular basis. Decide that you're not going to allow negative people to determine how you think, feel, and behave. Take back your power and focus your time and energy on becoming your best self.

# CONCLUSION

Y OU HEARD IT BEFORE. "You attract what you want". Actually not really, you can only attract who you are. If you notice your cycle is full of people you don't want to be around of, make some simple changes, also changing the movie you are playing in your mind on a daily basis. Start attracting who you want to be around to help you create the foundation of your career, to build the life you want. Do the work, and expect some good results. Take out the people that are draining you, that put you down, that do not share your vision. Attract who you want to become in your life. Start the purge today.

When you begin reading and thinking about the Law of Attraction, one of the first things that you discover is that positivity is of paramount importance. As you work to attract the thing you want; whether it's love, abundance, career advancement or health; you need to vibrate on a positive frequency if you're going to succeed. This is the same when you are attracting positive people into your life.

There are plenty of tools you can use to enhance your personal positivity. From keeping a daily gratitude journal to creating a dream board that displays images connected to joy and well-being.

However, the truth is that it isn't just your own positivity that matters. The vibration of others around you can also influence your likelihood of manifesting the life you desire. When you're surrounded by positive people, your self-esteem grows and you're in a constant feedback loop of excitement, inspiration, and energy.

If, on the other hand, you have negative people around you, then they can sap your positivity and make you vibrate on a lower frequency.

So, how do you ensure that you have as many positive people around you as possible?

## Use Visualization.

You'll already be familiar with the process of using creative visualization to build detailed, lifelike images of the things you want to attract. However, once you've honed your visualization skills, you can also use them to do other exercises.

One technique that can help you to attract positive people involves visualizing these people coming towards you. After you've focused on slow, steady breathing for a few minutes, allow your mind to generate an image that represents your ability to pull other positive people towards you.

## Target Your Own Negativity.

As the Law of Attraction states, we tend to attract more of the things we "give out" to the universe. So, if you're sending out negativity then it will be so much harder to attract positive people.

This negativity doesn't have to be malicious—for example, even if you are an accepting a friendly person, if you believe that you don't deserve positive people in your life then you're less likely to receive them.

Ask yourself whether you have any negative beliefs or assumptions about friendships and relationships. Then work to counter those in order to draw more positive people towards you.

## Be Honest.

Sometimes, we hold onto old friendships and relationships that are no longer working for us and only drag us down. To maximize your chances of meeting positive people and making solid connections, practice regular self-reflection about your social circle.

Is anyone dragging you down? Is there someone who always criticizes you, or even laughs at you? It's time to consider cutting ties with these sorts of people to make space for ones who will empower you and help you to reach your full potential.

## Give Love Every Day.

You can attract more positive people towards you if you're constantly radiating positivity even to strangers. Make a habit of giving love every day, and you'll see it begin to come back to you.

You don't have to make grand gestures even just complimenting someone on their gorgeous outfit, lending an ear to a troubled colleague for 20 minutes or giving an hour of your time to volunteer work each week can make a big difference. As a bonus, these types of activities may trigger wonderful new friendships!

## Practice affirmations before Socializing.

Finally, you can help to get yourself into the right headspace for making positive connections by giving yourself a bit of a pep talk before you socialize. Whether you're going to spending time getting to know people at work, going to a party or attending a dinner, try to find affirmations that make you feel open and happy about the possibility of getting to know people.

Focus on your most positive qualities and the things that you know other people appreciate about you. Reaffirm your belief in these aspects of yourself. For example, you might say "I feel and trust the positive energy inside me" or "I have the power to attract positive people who will enrich my life."

# I WILL MIND MY LIFE FROM THIS DAY ON...

*Today is the day I decide to be outstanding.*

*I also decide to start fresh.*

*I decide to have a clear path to my destination.*

*I am only focusing on my strengths and leave behind my weaknesses.*

*I am embracing my fears and I am my own boss.*

*I am who I am and I love me.*

*I know there is greatness in me, I will no longer seat in this corner watching others takeoff and wonder when will my time come.*

*This day is mine. I am rising to the top. I am claiming my victory.*

*I'm, I can, and I will succeed.*

# ABOUT THE AUTHOR

Moirar M. Leveille, is a Licensed Mental Health Counselor, a Strategic Intervention Life Coach and Neuro Linguistic Practitioner. She is the CEO of Mind Time, LLC, where she provides Life Coaching in French, Spanish, Creole, and Portuguese, locally and internationally, to help individuals achieve their goals in short-term. Moirar provides Mental Health Counseling, in a non-profit organization, to a very diverse population to manage their emotions, dealing with trauma, depression, anxiety, addiction, and mental illness of all sorts. Moirar is well known for her dedication, charisma, her "joie de vivre" and her desire to help others remove their own limits to achieve success and live in an optimal state of mind to create their happiness. She is a resident of Nantucket in the state of Massachusetts.

# NEXT STEPS

What does it take to live in your own terms?
Are you happy with your accomplishments so far?
Do you have a clear vision to where you are going in life?

To move on from where you are to fulfillment, you need commitment, persistence, courage, determination, and passion.

This is a book of life to help you take control of your now to move on to the best part of your life. Just open your mind to new experiences.

## 1. JOIN THE COMMUNITY

Visit mindtimecoaching.com to get more information on how to get personalize help and have access to other tools.

## 2. SHARE THIS BOOK

Please write a review on Amazon and tell others who you think will enjoy this book. Spreading the word helps to reach new readers, grow this movement and the continued production of similar content. Click here to write a review.

THANK YOU FOR YOUR SUPPORT